Mother's Daughter

ALSO BY KATE HENNIG

The Last Wife
The Virgin Trial
Cyrano de Bergerac

MOTHER'S DAUGHTER

Kate Hennig

**PLAYWRIGHTS
CANADA PRESS**

Toronto

Playwrights Canada Press
202-269 Richmond St. W., Toronto, ON M5V 1X1
416.703.0013 :: info@playwrightscanada.com :: www.playwrightscanada.com

LIBRARY AND ARCHIVES CANADA CATALOGUING IN PUBLICATION
Title: Mother's daughter / Kate Hennig.
Names: Hennig, Kate, author.
Description: First edition. | A play.
Identifiers: Canadiana (print) 20190116242 | Canadiana (ebook) 2019011813X | ISBN 9780369100115 (softcover) | ISBN 9780369100122 (PDF) | ISBN 9780369100139 (EPUB) | ISBN 9780369100146 (Kindle)
Subjects: LCSH: Mary I, Queen of England, 1516-1558—Drama.
Classification: LCC PS8615.E543 M68 2019 | DDC C812/.6—dc23

Playwrights Canada Press acknowledges that we operate on land, which, for thousands of years, has been the traditional territories of the Mississaugas of the Credit First Nation, Huron-Wendat, Anishinaabe, Métis, and Haudenosaunee peoples. Today, this meeting place is home to many Indigenous peoples from across Turtle Island and we are grateful to have the opportunity to work and play here.

We acknowledge the financial support of the Canada Council for the Arts—which last year invested $153 million to bring the arts to Canadians throughout the country—the Ontario Arts Council (OAC), Ontario Creates, and the Government of Canada for our publishing activities.

To my childhood friend, Hilary Beaton, for her
kindred spirit, creative support, and for all the
years of laughter we have shared.

And to Bob White, for his dedication, his wisdom,
and his prodigious contribution to the art of writing for theatre in Canada.

This is an *imagining* of history. Oh yes, it is based on actual people and events, and though portions of it are deliciously accurate, some may offend the historically concise among you, while still others are completely and utterly fabricated. My priority in choosing must always favour the dramatic.

What I am deeply interested in is the humanity of these iconic historical characters. I want to imagine what made them do what they did, just as I want to imagine what made Margaret Thatcher, Donald Trump, and Bashar al-Assad do what they did. They are human after all. They have mothers, fathers, siblings, and children. One expects that they play tennis, watch television, read books; they laugh, worry, drink too much coffee from time to time. It fascinates me to create these personal possibilities, and then imagine how they might lead to some of the major decisions that history records. It calls our political self-righteousness into question.

This is a contemporary play. This is a domestic play. No historical costuming or accents required. Diversity in casting is strongly encouraged. This is Mary's story.

—KH

Mother's Daughter was first produced by the Stratford Festival and premiered at the Studio Theatre in Stratford, Ontario, on June 14, 2019, with the following cast and creative team:

Bassett: Beryl Bain
Bess and Anne: Jessica B. Hill
Catalina: Irene Poole
Jane: Andrea Rankin
Mary: Shannon Taylor
Susan: Maria Vacratsis
Simon: Gordon Patrick White

Director: Alan Dilworth
Designer: Lorenzo Savoini
Lighting Designer: Kimberly Purtell
Sound Designer: Debashis Sinha
Dramaturge: Bob White
Fight Director: Anita Nittoly
Assistant Costume Designer: Julia Holbert
Assistant Lighting Designer: Logan Raju Cracknell
Stage Manager: Kim Lott
Assistant Stage Manager: Katherine Arcus
Production Assistant: Emma Slunt
Production Stage Managers: Marie Fewer, Kim Lott, and Maxwell T. Wilson
Technical Director: Sean Hirtle

Artistic Director: Antoni Cimolino
Executive Director: Anita Gaffney
Producer: David Auster
Casting Director: Beth Russell
Creative Planning Director: Jason Miller

Mother's Daughter was originally commissioned and produced by the Stratford Festival. The initial stage of this work was created during a residency in the Leighton Artists Studios at the Banff Centre for Arts and Creativity. Support for the creation of *Mother's Daughter* was generously provided by the Foerster Bernstein New Play Development Program and by Charles Beall and Karon Bales.

PLAYWRIGHT'S NOTES

From the essay "A Change in Appearance," first published in the Stratford Festival program for the premiere of *Mother's Daughter*.

I was listening to *As It Happens* on CBC Radio the other night. One of the guests was a professor from a Barcelona university who had been granted 2.3 million dollars to research early women's writing. She is certainly not the first person to embark on this endeavour—many people have been unearthing the work of early female artists and writers over the past thirty years or so—but, by creating a context with enormous numbers of individual works, Carme Font Paz plans to recognize the contribution of these women to the history of ideas. Even though they have been dead for nearly five hundred years, they will have an opportunity to *reappear*.

I want that for Mary.

Even if I don't have 2.3 million dollars.

Do you know who Rebecca Solnit is? Pick up one of her books or read one of her contributions to the *Guardian* or *Harper's* Easy Chair. She writes about women, the environment, hope, community, politics, walking . . . things like that. She said this in her essay, *Men Explain Things to Me* (my italics): "Every woman who *appears* wrestles with the forces that would have her *disappear*. She struggles with the forces that would tell her story for her, or write her out of the story, the genealogy, the rights of man, the rule of law. The ability to tell your own story, in words or images, is already a victory, already a revolt."

Now, let me tell you about the *appearance* of a dove:

In 2017, just before rehearsals began for *The Virgin Trial*, I went to England. My childhood friend Hilary and I spent several days of laughter and storytelling, hitting many notable locations frequented by the characters in my plays. I called our holiday the Katherine Parr Trail.

We started at Eddie's favourite house, Hunsdon, which is only seven kilometres from the little town where Hilary and I were born. We then went south and west into the glorious green of Gloucestershire to see Sudeley Castle, the home of Thomas Seymour and of Parr's velvet lined toilet. Then to the Bodleian Library at Oxford to see the actual book that Elizabeth had written for Parr: the book Bess gives to Kate in *The Last Wife*. We went to Kendal and met with the lord mayor and saw Parr's prayer book (the one carried by Jane Grey as her chief mourner). We went across the Yorkshire Dales to Snape Castle and to the magnificent Tudor house, Gainsborough Old Hall, two of Parr's marital residences.

All these places—all these objects—hold the stories of the women in my plays. I could feel them somehow: through these ways of touching time, their lives reappeared.

Before we got to Elizabeth's stomping grounds at Hatfield, a favourite day was spent in the town of Framlingham, where Mary was named the first queen of England. While I was walking the ramparts of the cold and formidable castle, still adorned by a series of designer Tudor chimneys, a pure white dove flew over my head and nestled on a little rock ledge only feet from me. I stopped. I didn't move. Nor did the dove. It looked at me. I looked at it. Several minutes passed. Then I said . . . "I'll do my best."

There's something about Mary . . . She is not triumphant like her sister, Elizabeth. She is not ambitious, like Katherine Parr. Mary is not a martyr, like Jane Grey. Mary is not a hero.

Maybe that's why it has been so easy for history to vilify her across the ages, to demonize her as a religious fundamentalist who was the enemy of humanism and reason, the enemy of Gloriana, the Virgin

Queen. Few people even distinguish her from her cousin, Mary Queen of Scots! Mary has been written into history as the bad guy.

Now, I'm not saying she's a good guy. Mary's just human. Or at least in my plays I am contemplating her humanity.

It's been a tough journey, for me: writing this play, trying to satisfy that little white dove. That's probably because Mary's story is so magnificently complex, there's enough material for three plays (I've thrown out over thirty thousand words!!): from her survival as an infant when her parents' other child-bearing attempts failed, to the personal grief she felt when the English lost Calais, their last stronghold on the continent. Mary's life was surrounded by bitter disappointment.

Mary is the child of a nasty divorce; a child raised in riches and glory, only to end up an employee in her half-sister's nursery; a devout young woman whose religion was outlawed by her father and then by her brother; a young woman who was constantly, and ineffectively, bartered by her father for political gain; a young woman who was refused access to her dying mother; a young woman who was forced to sign a document denying the lawful marriage of her parents, and thereby her own legitimacy; a woman who chose to marry a man who didn't love her; a woman who had two phantom pregnancies, the second one—likely cancer—resulting in her death. A queen whose governmental policies were responsible for the death of 283 religious dissenters.

At the same time, Mary was a woman who took on a job that no woman ever had before; she wore her father's robes at her coronation because no robes had ever been made for a woman; she had a bill passed through parliament that allowed women who wore the crown to be equal in power to their male counterparts. And if you are ever in question of her courage, just take a look at the pre-nuptial agreement she negotiated with Philip II: Mary had balls.

So, in helping Mary to *appear*, I want the word "bloody" to *disappear*. Even if I know that Mary is not the pure white dove, I also know that appearance and reality are married in complex and inexplicable ways.

Bess and Anne should always be portrayed by the same actor.

A forward slash (/) indicates the next speaker should overlap their dialogue at the slash; when this occurs at the beginning of the line, the next speaker completely overlaps that line.

An em dash (—) at the end of a line indicates that the thought should be cut off, either by the current speaker or by the next speaker jumping in.

An ellipsis (. . .) indicates that the speaker should search briefly for the thought, leaving a gap in speech.

Square brackets ([ ]) surrounding dialogue indicates the the unspoken end of the thought.

*Every woman who appears wrestles with the forces
that would have her disappear. She struggles with the
forces that would tell her story for her, or write her out
of the story, the genealogy, the rights of man, the rule
of law. The ability to tell your own story, in words or
images, is already a victory, already a revolt.*
—Rebecca Solnit, *Men Explain Things to Me*

*In certain things she is singular and without an equal;
for not only is she brave and valiant, unlike other
timid and spiritless women, but so courageous and
resolute, that neither in adversity nor peril did she ever
display or commit any act of cowardice or pusillanimity, maintaining always, on the contrary, a wonderful
grandeur and dignity . . . it cannot be denied that she
shows herself to have been born of a truly royal lineage.*
—Venetian Ambassador Giovanni Michieli on
Mary I of England

*She's a Killer Queen
Gunpowder, gelatin
Dynamite with a laser beam
Guaranteed to blow your mind
Anytime*
—Queen, "Killer Queen"

CHARACTERS

Mary: a princess, thirty-eight years old; *private, cutting, wounded, capable, loyal; water*

Bess: a princess, twenty years old; *intelligent, precocious, entitled, unedited, sexual; fire*

Anne: a mother quean, thirty-two years old; *patient, determined, destructive, flamboyant, ambitious; fire*

Catalina: a mother queen, forty-eight years old; *authoritative, traditional, embittered, constant, narcissistic; earth*

Jane: a disciple, sixteen years old; *intuitive, righteous, naive, disciplined, myopic; air*

Susan: a defender, fifty-eight years old; *protective, goading, fearful, devoted, xenophobic; earth*

Bassett: a strategist, thirty-two years old; *progressive, bookish, industrious, alluring, wily; water*

Simon: a diplomat, forty years old; *impatient, assertive, stoical, elitist, slippery; water*

ACT ONE
EDDIE'S DEVISE

In private. A storm is raging outside. Two cloaked figures rush in.

BESS *(fuming)* It is *so* your fault!

MARY Why? Why is it my fault?

BESS I've been thrown out with your bathwater!

MARY I've been thrown out, too, you / know.

BESS We all knew that would happen.

MARY Did we.

BESS Eddie hated you. He hated everything you stand for. But me? I'm the *temperate* sister!

MARY You're proud of what your grovelling earns / you?

BESS *(indicating with her finger and thumb)* I was *this close* to getting what I wanted.

MARY Say it. I dare you.

BESS Legal acces/sion.

MARY Unbeliev/able.

BESS Now he's tied us together and given us *both* the boot!

MARY Just—hurry up, will ya? Dudley and his posse are on their way.

BESS You think he knows I'm here? Hah! Not a chance: I look over my shoulder. He wouldn't be coming here if you'd turned yourself in.

MARY Shut up and show me.

BESS Here.

BESS takes a document from inside her cloak.

"My devise for the succession. By Edward the King."

MARY *(to BESS, with some distrust)* How'd you get it?

BESS Favours.

BESS reads from the document.

"For lack of issue male of my body, the succession shall fall to the male heirs of Lady Frances Grey: niece to the late King Henry. For lack of such issue, the succession shall fall to her daughter, the Lady Jane Grey—"

MARY *(incredulous)* And there it is—

BESS "—and the *male heirs* of the said Lady Jane."

MARY Little Jane Grey.

BESS "I drank the Kool-Aid" Jane Grey; "I just married Dudley's stupid son Guildford" Jane Grey.
It's not even subtle: Guildford marries Jane, Jane becomes Queen, Dudley stands on top of the cake.

BESS points to the document.

An impressive strategy, don't you think?

MARY *(squeezing it in)* No.

BESS   All Jane's male heirs are also *Dudley's* male heirs. That's the icing.

> *BESS is obsessed, flipping through pages of the document.*

But Eddie doesn't stop there. Look: Jane's younger sisters come next, the kids of Jane's kids, the kids of Jane's sisters' kids. Basically anyone related to Jane . . . but us.

MARY   Me. Anyone but me.

> *MARY takes the document from BESS. BESS is still over her shoulder.*

> *BESS points out a spot in the document.*

BESS   "The *illegitimate, half-blood relatives* are, for all intents and purposes, disabled to ask, claim, or challenge for the said imperial crown."

MARY   Who's the bastard.

BESS   May he rest in peace.

> *MARY and BESS consider this.*

MARY   Jane Grey is gonna be the first queen of England.

BESS   Yes. Well. You're not really equipped.

MARY   For the love / of—!

BESS   *(honestly)* Nothing against you, but it was Father's *personality* that kept the country together, not his policy, and personality's not exactly your strong suit.

MARY   Does your lack of tact / even—

BESS   Without a charismatic leader, polarization is all this country will ever know.

MARY   Oh, so your charisma can heal our religious divisions?

BESS   Our *political* divisions. Almost certainly. Better than yours can. I am the popular choice.

MARY	You make me nuts.
BESS	You should be worrying about Dudley now, not me. He's going to get Jane on the throne. And *this (the document)* supports both his religion and his politics.

SUSAN and BASSETT interrupt.

SUSAN	*(to MARY)* Bassett insists we ride tonight!
BASSETT	*(to SUSAN)* Because you'd be happy waffling until it's too late.
MARY	We're going, Susan.
SUSAN	*(recalcitrantly)* Sure, don't listen to / me.
BASSETT	If we push it, we can hit Framlingham by mid-morning.
MARY	Let's push it—
SUSAN	Dudley won't / raise a hand to you—
MARY	—before his cowboys arrive.
BESS	You're gonna do it, then? Seize the crown?
MARY	*You* would be seizing the crown. I will take my rightful place, thank you very much.
SUSAN	God willing.
BESS	So, what're you gonna do with Jane?
MARY	She's less of a threat than you are.
BASSETT	/ She's a blasphemer.
SUSAN	/ She's a usurper.
BESS	She's a cognate.
MARY	She's a kid. So she goes to a different church; so she has some . . . newfangled political ideas; she's still entitled to justice.

They all look at MARY.

She is. I taught her how to play hopscotch.

BESS	She just put her foot down on your square!
MARY	So—what—I should blast her out of the playground?
BASSETT	/ Probably.
SUSAN	/ Possibly.
BESS	Yes!
MARY	Jane / is—
BESS	Jane is / the—
MARY	Shut up, shut up, shut up: I get it. Jane is the first order of business.

MARY turns, then turns back.

Hey. Hasn't Dudley sent for you, too?

BESS	Out of sight, out of mind: I'm going to Hatfield. *(hands on belly)* A female complaint.
MARY	Really?
BESS	The best possible excuse for not doing what you're told.

MARY puts a hand on her own belly. The storm outside blows.

MARY	*(to SUSAN and BASSETT)* Let's get the hell out of Dodge.

SUSAN and BASSETT go. BESS hurries away in the opposite direction.

BESS	See you, Mary.
MARY	See you, Bess.

LIMBO

In between. MARY *turns to see the full figure of a woman in silhouette. We can't make out her features. Is she a goddess? MARY stares. The figure seems to return her gaze, though we are unable to see her eyes.*

MARY   Hi. Hi, there. What's—?
Can I help you?

CATALINA   Am I not here to help you?

MARY   Holy. Shit.

CATALINA   Language.

MARY   Sorry, sorry, I'm so / sorry.

CATALINA   I have always been here when you need me.

MARY   Need you? I—
Do I—?

CATALINA steps out of the shadows.

Oh.

CATALINA   Is it better? To look me in the eye?

MARY   I don't— Uh. No. Not . . .

CATALINA   You want my help.

MARY   I guess . . .

CATALINA   You must act *now*. Do it.

MARY   Do . . . what.

CATALINA   Provide the proof.

MARY   Of . . . ?

CATALINA   That the eleven years I spent fighting for my marriage were not in vain.

MARY	Whoa, Ma—hang on a sec—how does dredging up your marriage help *me*? There are a few more pressing issues around here / and—
CATALINA	*(disappointed)* Are you incapable, then?
MARY	*(mothers)* Here we go—
CATALINA	My great-great-grandmother, my great-grandmother—
MARY	Ma—
CATALINA	—my grandmother: all queens . . .
MARY	—oh boy—
CATALINA	My mother, my sister for whom you are named: also queens. We are descended from queens of Castile, from queens of Aragon, from Edward III—
MARY	*(under her breath)* He was a queen?
CATALINA	Always the clown.
MARY	Ha. No. Not for a long time. I stopped making people laugh years uh-go-I-wow-you . . . make me nervous. Mamá! You make me so nervous!
CATALINA	*(impatient with MARY's joke)* I had more right to the English throne than your father ever had. It was my blood, the blood that pulsed through the veins of all those queens, / that validated the Tudor claim to the throne—
MARY	*(by rote)* . . . that validated the Tudor claim to the throne. See. It's not like I've forgotten you.
CATALINA	—the combined blood of England and Spain, that stirs in you now.
MARY	*(her belly)* Oh. Is that what this—?
CATALINA	Prove that your father was wrong.

MARY	Many times, about many things. Even Henry would say that.
CATALINA	Eleven and a half years he chose to humiliate me, because he could not get a son—
MARY	I've heard it before—
CATALINA	You are his rightful heir.
MARY	Yup: I'm his heir. I was always his heir.
CATALINA	Trained to be Queen / from the moment of your birth.
MARY	From the moment of my birth.
CATALINA	All others are pretenders.

MARY waits to see if the onslaught will continue.

MARY	And this is helping me how, again?
CATALINA	You must kill the pretenders.
MARY	*(amused)* That might be . . . overreacting a bit, don't ya think?
CATALINA	You must kill your cousin and the bastard you call sister.
MARY	Hah!

CATALINA is determined.

CATALINA	Mary.
MARY	Mamá.
CATALINA	Kill them both.
MARY	No way. I don't think so. I'm not gonna kill little Jane Grey. And though on occasion I might like to, I can't kill Bess.
CATALINA	How else will you prove that your father was wrong to disinherit you? How else will you redeem me?
MARY	Something less . . . malevolent, / perhaps—?

CATALINA   My name. My marriage. My *faith*.

            This gives MARY *pause.*

            Mi ratóncita. I need you to do this for *me*.
            They are heretics. Both of them.

MARY   You see, so is half the country then. You want me to kill
            half the country?

CATALINA   *(not amused)* You must take your rightful place as Queen.
            You must bear an heir to both England and Empire.
            The pretenders stand in your way.

MARY   / But—

CATALINA   Never talk back to me.
            Begin with your cousin.

            CATALINA *withdraws into the shadows.* MARY *is left
            perplexed.*

ACTION MOVIE 1—
FIRST STRIKE FROM FRAMLINGHAM

            *At table. Preparations for war are underway. A large map
            of England is laid out on the table, showing France, Spain,
            and the English Channel.* SUSAN *is looking out the window
            at a yard below.* MARY *stands, holding a slanderous broad-
            sheet that she's been reading.*

SUSAN   It's getting crowded out there.

            SUSAN, *seeing the broadsheet, takes it.*

            Oh, for pity's sake, don't read that garbage: it has nothing
            to do with anything.

MARY   The whole country's reading it.

SUSAN   A few people in London are reading it. One self-important town is not the whole country.

> *SUSAN crumples up the paper. BASSETT enters.*

MARY   Bassett! What's the word?

> *BASSETT places a report in front of MARY.*

BASSETT   The Treasury and the Tower have fallen to Dudley—

MARY   / Eee.

BASSETT   —and now he's stockpiling weapons to defend the new queen.

SUSAN   NOT the new / queen.

BASSETT   The Lady Jane.

MARY   Is he sending someone after us?

BASSETT   No—

SUSAN   *(under BASSETT)* Phew.

BASSETT   —he's coming himself—

SUSAN   *(under BASSETT)* / Criminy.

BASSETT   —infantry and cavalry in tow.

MARY   How close?

BASSETT   Past Cambridge. Only just. According to the scout.

> *BASSETT takes a notepad and pencil and makes some calculations.*

SUSAN   He's a reasonable man, you know, Dudley. He might be lenient with you / if you—

> *MARY looks over BASSETT's shoulder at the report.*

MARY   With what kind of numbers?

BASSETT   *(reading from the report)* A thousand on horse, three-thousand on foot, twelve cannons, thirty carts of ammunition.

BASSETT makes an adjustment on the report.

SUSAN   Well, we certainly can't compete with / that kind of—

BASSETT   If they break to rest and eat we have about eighteen hours. A day at most.

MARY   And our side?

SUSAN   It is getting crowded out there.

BASSETT   A bunch of local farmers in the yard.

MARY   Excellent.

BASSETT   *(in the report)* Also . . . something in here about the location of the French . . . *(finding it)* Dudley's sent five warships down from Yarmouth—

MARY   / Lordy.

SUSAN   / Five!

BASSETT   —that'll soon have free passage to the coastline . . . just . . . *(points on the map)* here, because the French fleet—

MARY   *(figuring it out)* / Shit.

BASSETT   —are blocking access to the North Sea, just . . . here *(pointing on the map)*, holding back any support you might have coming up from Spain.

SUSAN   We've gotta run, Mouse. If we go north we can / cross at—

BASSETT   Susan!
         (to MARY) Dudley won't let you get out of England alive.

SUSAN   Surrender then. What choice do we have?

BASSETT makes adjustments on the map.

MARY   Five warships.

BASSETT   A substantial show of force.

SUSAN	Dudley'll crush your faithful farmers, take you prisoner, then chop off your head!
MARY	Doesn't have half my charm.
SUSAN	A lot of good your charm will have against his brute squad.
BASSETT	I say go brute against brute. Make the first strike. Take Dudley out.
MARY	/ You think—?
SUSAN	*(commenting on that plan)* Or, just give me a gun and I'll shoot you myself.
MARY	*(adamant)* We can't stand up to him with our motley crew.
BASSETT	Why not? Because you wear a skirt? Don't let him get away with that. Be like Kate.
MARY	Kate.
BASSETT	Parr. She stood up to Henry. Stood up to his whole Council when she was regent.
MARY	The Council weren't armed with twelve cannons.
BASSETT	We take our chances.
SUSAN	*(to BASSETT)* And risk the life of the rightful queen?!
BASSETT	*(to SUSAN)* Or sit here and wait for them to arrive? Damn it, Susan: try to be useful / instead of—
SUSAN	Just because you've worked for four queens does not give you the right to speak to me / like I'm—
BASSETT	*(lording it)* Five. Soon / enough.
MARY	Oh, quit your bickering!

BASSETT and SUSAN retreat to their respective corners.

BASSETT	*(to MARY)* If we get Dudley, the rest of the hounds'll be called off.

SUSAN *(to MARY)* If he gets *you*, it's exile at best, imprisonment—
execution more likely.

MARY *(going for it)* In for a penny, in for a pound.

SUSAN *(the martyrdom begins)* Well then, I'd like to say I've enjoyed
the thirty-eight years I got to spend with / you—

MARY *(to BASSETT)* Should I give orders?

SUSAN *(throwing in the towel)* Completely unreasonable.

    BASSETT waves the notepad and pen.

BASSETT Paper. Ready. Right here.

MARY *(an order)* Commence the march on Dudley tomorrow at
dawn. We'll leave a selection of the feisty farmers to defend
the castle just so's we've got somewhere to retreat when we
turn our petticoats and run.

    MARY looks to SUSAN for support.

SUSAN Me? I wash my hands.

MARY *(to BASSETT)* Take it, then! Go on! Shoo!

BASSETT *(a battle cry)* ALALA!

    BASSETT exits with the order. MARY watches BASSETT go.
    Her tone changes.

MARY You could help with the plan, you know, instead of just
telling me to leg it, or moping in the corner.

SUSAN You don't know what you're doing!

MARY Thanks.

SUSAN Well, do you? You've never gone to war!

MARY I know, I know, you think I don't know?! I can't run for the
hills, okay? I can't. I've gotta fight. If I'm gonna be Queen,
it can't be about which sparkly dress I'm wearing to the ball.

SUSAN Don't you patronize me, young lady—

MARY	If we win tomorrow, we prove my divine right.
SUSAN	And if we lose?
MARY	Don't jinx it! I was *born* to be queen. Just ask my mother.
SUSAN	If your mother was here I'd ask her why she didn't put "armed combat" in the princess training manual.
MARY	*(the bright side)* But, hey: gambling wasn't top of her list either, and you taught me plenty about that.
SUSAN	Too much.
MARY	When the cards are crap . . . ?
SUSAN	You keep your head.
MARY	And if I don't?
SUSAN	You make poor decisions.
MARY	*(with penetrating doubt)* Can I win?
SUSAN	*(wagging her finger)* If you play clean and mean, the way I taught you.
MARY	*(grabbing SUSAN's finger)* I'll do my best.

MARY suddenly grasps her belly.

Ho.

BASSETT returns with a note in hand.

SUSAN	*(to MARY)* Y'okay?
MARY	I enjoy being a girl.
BASSETT	Things are looking up out there.
SUSAN	I said— But do you listen to / me? Nooo.
BASSETT	Not a very skilled force, mind you—
MARY	Isn't that what Dudley's expecting?
BASSETT	Well, he's sure not expecting to meet you on the road.

MARY	With my rustic cadre.
	Then the lightbulb moment:
	Hey, you guys . . .
SUSAN	What?
MARY	*(to BASSETT)* They serve the *crown*. All Dudley's infantry and cavalry and cannons, they don't serve *him*, right? They serve the crown.
SUSAN	Why. What.
MARY	Well, if the crown changes hands . . . shouldn't *they*?
BASSETT	*(considering)* I'm not sure we can rely / on that—
MARY	They're public servants. I'm my father's heir.
SUSAN	You certainly are.
BASSETT	*(the plan falls into place)* If you want to play it that way, then . . . we should put you out front. Don't you think? You should lead the attack.
MARY	I should, shouldn't I.
SUSAN	Oh, for the love— / Do you need your heads examined?!
BASSETT	They'll see Henry's child, with their old friends and colleagues behind / her . . .
SUSAN	*(to MARY)* You will not go out in front!
MARY	We gotta bet their allegiance will turn.
BASSETT	I'm in.
	I'll see your bet . . .
	BASSETT hands MARY the note, which MARY opens.
	And raise you . . .
MARY	*(looking up)* Fifteen thousand?!
SUSAN	But when *I* tell you, you don't listen.

MARY	*(looking for assurance)* *Fifteen thousand* local farmers?
BASSETT	Awaiting your inspection.
MARY	And they came here because of *me*?

SUSAN kneels in front of MARY, kisses her hand.

SUSAN	Regina christus tantum et / regina cordis mei.

BASSETT follows in short suit.

BASSETT	Regina christus tantum et / regina cordis mei.
MARY	*(getting them back on their feet)* Not yet. Not yet. Not until it's on my head. *(looking at SUSAN)* Susan: I need practical shoes. We're going down to the yard: I suddenly have *(waving the note)* a shit-load of local farmers to inspect!

THE SCHISM

In between. Time has passed. MARY stands alone. CATALINA appears carrying a robe over her arm.

CATALINA	Not much of a soldier, this Dudley: losing a battle to a woman.
MARY	*(still stunned)* The warships changed sides. The land troops laid down their weapons. Dudley declared me Queen right there on the road.
CATALINA	Ah: so, in fact, he conceded to you; you did not defeat him.
MARY	Thanks for pointing that out.
CATALINA	It was a miracle.
MARY	It kinda felt like one.
CATALINA	Your destiny, not your accomplishment.

MARY	Oh-kay.
CATALINA	Not everyone who aspires to the throne could achieve such a victory.
MARY	And . . . would you like to put it any other way?
CATALINA	You did not attain it. God intervened on your behalf.
MARY	That about sums it up then.

CATALINA helps MARY into the robe.

CATALINA	It is not Elizabeth who will be crowned today.
MARY	Nope.
CATALINA	Nor the pretender Jane Grey.
MARY	Mmmhmm.
CATALINA	They are not fit in the eyes of God.
MARY	Let's not mince words.
CATALINA	You have achieved this secular title. Now you must secure it. You must restore the faith of your people. Restore the salvation of their souls.
MARY	I . . . will get to that, yes.
CATALINA	Heed me, Maria. Unity provides security. One marriage. One faith. You must repair the schism that your father created. The schism that killed me and shattered you.
MARY	Uh-huh—
CATALINA	The schism that bore the bastard Elizabeth. The schism that led to the pretender Jane.
MARY	I can't. Seriously. I can't put those pieces back together. That's asking too much of anyone.
CATALINA	It's not too much for a queen.
MARY	*(maybe whining a little)* My kid brother has—

CATALINA *(under her breath)* Bastardo.

MARY —been on the throne for seven years, and his foreign and domestic policy was a perfect storm. I have the practicalities of his disastrous legacy to repair first.

CATALINA Are you complaining?

MARY *(yes)* No.

CATALINA Then you will do it.

MARY I appreciate your confidence.

CATALINA Eliminate the political opposition. Restore the one true faith.

MARY Simple-dimple.
You know, I have a hunch Dudley knew exactly what he was doing, making Jane the first queen of this kingdom. He pushed her up there because he knew there was no way she could succeed, and when she fell, he'd be right there to say I told you so.

CATALINA You will not fall; you will not fail. You will do what is necessary. You have *me* beside you, not Dudley. Jane was not granted the throne. You were. You have no choice now but to succeed.

And CATALINA is gone.

In private. MARY *stands on the table in a traditional crimson surcoat made for Henry VIII's coronation. She is distant.* BASSETT *is at the table with her feet up, her nose in a book.* SUSAN *has a series of sketches of the coronation robes nearby and shows them to* MARY *as she finishes hemming the surcoat* MARY *is wearing.*

SUSAN   *(doubtfully)* The archbishop puts on the white tunic—

BASSETT   The anointing gown first.

SUSAN   *(a bit snippy)* This is after the anointing.

> SIMON *enters with his agenda. He bows very formally.*

BASSETT   Suit yourself.

SIMON   Your Majesty.

MARY   Hi, Simon.

SIMON   *(uncomfortably)* The . . . briefing, Your Majesty.

MARY   *(coming back from another planet)* Sorry. I was— I'm . . . dressing.

SIMON   Dressing? W— oh. Uh. A screen could perhaps be provided . . .

MARY   Not *un*dressing, Simon. Just . . . adding more. Or . . . figuring out what they're going to add . . . / once . . .

SUSAN   Over the crimson surcoat goes the . . .

> SUSAN *looks for the sketch.*

BASSETT   White tunic.

SIMON   Matters of state, Your Majesty: the audience should go.

SUSAN   The audience?

MARY	They're fine.
SIMON	If Your Majesty will allow me to instruct you in the established protocols: the sovereign and his am/bassador—
MARY	Her.
SIMON	—take private meetings.
BASSETT	We're fine.

SIMON raises an eyebrow at this. He lays a file on the table.

SIMON	Language is hereby drafted to confirm the validity of your parents' marriage, and thereby your legitimacy as the one true and legal inheritrix of the realm.
SUSAN	*(impressed)* Inheritrix.
BASSETT	Nice touch.
SUSAN	Your mother went to her grave in the hope of that.
MARY	Then let's pray she's finally happy. Legitimate. Tick. Next?

SIMON makes a tick on his agenda.

SUSAN	*(showing a sketch)* The supertunic.
SIMON	*(another document)* As requested, I've outlined the proposed religious settlement with no mention of the pope.
BASSETT	No—? Hang on. Why wouldn't you / mention—?
MARY	Gradually. With the religion / stuff.
SIMON	*(to BASSETT)* I am a diplomat. *You* are a member of the household staff.
SUSAN	The supertunic is fastened with the sword belt, then replaced later by / the . . .

SUSAN, again, looks for the sketch.

BASSETT	*(to SUSAN)* The purple surcoat and the imperial robe.

	(back to MARY*)* The Catholic court has been in exile for six years. They expect you to turn things around.
SUSAN	Just 'cause you haven't had a job in all that time—
MARY	I want to be reasonable. I'm going to be reasonable.
BASSETT	Eddie wasn't reasonable.
MARY	If we keep wiping out everything the previous government put in place how are we gonna get anywhere?
SIMON	Reversal in policy is considered a show of strength.
BASSETT	I / agree.

        SIMON clears his throat.

SIMON	As do the old families you've brought back onto Council.
MARY	*(to* SIMON*)* I thought you were supporting me on the moderate approach.
SIMON	I have no opinion, Your Majesty. I merely present a range of possibilities.
BASSETT	The old Catholic families want their land back.
MARY	It was never their land to begin with. It was the Church's land. Restoring land to elite Catholic families has nothing to do with restoring land to the Church. It's political patronage.
BASSETT	*(with fire in her belly)* Come. On. It's not / [political patronage].
SIMON	*(agreeing with* MARY*)* May I suggest a temperate policy: keep Rome at a distance in the first parliament and leave the disputed lands with the Protestants for the time being.
MARY	There.
SUSAN	How would your mother feel about that?
MARY	My mother was queen of the long game.

SIMON	*(back to his clipboard)* No mention of the pope.
BASSETT	For now.
MARY	Church. Tick. Next.

SIMON *makes a tick on his agenda.*

SIMON	National security issues.
SUSAN	On coronation day?
MARY	I'm not even sitting in the chair for another— How much longer, Bassett?

BASSETT *checks her watch.*

BASSETT	One hour and seventeen minutes.
MARY	*(her stomach)* Sheesh. Them's some big butterflies.
SIMON	We are very fortunate that the transfer of power is going so smoothly, but there are rebellious factions still very much at large. Your sister being one.
MARY	My sister is supporting my claim.
SIMON	The Lady Elizabeth is currently at liberty to do as she pleases.
BASSETT	That goes for Henry Grey. And Jane Grey, too.
SUSAN	*(defending MARY)* Jane Grey is not "at liberty": she's locked in the tower! You're just trying to stir up the shit.
SIMON	The Grey girl should be executed. Routine policy.
MARY	Not my routine.
SUSAN	*(still on the shit-stirring)* For pity's sake.
MARY	Why is everyone so riled up because I won't kill Jane Grey?
SUSAN	Yeah: she's a sweet little girl who came to her auntie's house every week for tea. The *public* don't care a noodle about Jane Grey.

MARY	Exactly: *I'm the guy.* You couldn't hear yourself think for all the partying that went on when I was proclaimed Queen. The people want *me. All* the people.
SUSAN	Well, really, they want your father. But you're the closest thing.

MARY looks sideways at SUSAN.

MARY	*(to SIMON)* How does killing Jane Grey win me any points with the Council?
BASSETT	It shows the conservative allies that you care about your traditional base. Kill the girl. It'll buy you some wiggle room around the land rights issues.
SIMON	It will set a deterrent for your sister.
MARY	No. I'm gonna cut Jane loose.
SIMON	Too much mercy.
MARY	*(adamant)* I will not kill my cousin! The end! Clemency. Tick. What else?

SIMON makes an "x" on his agenda.

SUSAN picks up a picture of . . .

SUSAN	The coronation spoon.
SIMON	With respect, I reiterate the question of Elizabeth, Your Majesty.
BASSETT	*(too casually)* If she won't deal with Jane, she's sure not gonna deal / with—
MARY	*(in BASSETT's face)* Hey! Cut it out! I'm making decisions about peoples' lives!

MARY has a sudden pain in her belly. She winces and bites her lip. CATALINA appears, unseen by all but MARY.

Shit.

SUSAN *(to BASSETT)* Look what you've done! She has to stand on that balcony for how many hours this afternoon?

BASSETT *(to MARY)* I overstepped.

MARY You just . . . got my goat. Which is chewing up the lining of my stomach, apparently.
Bess, Simon. What about her?

SIMON Your sister has a history of devious intent.

SUSAN *(facetiously)* Really . . .

SIMON You might consider detaining her.

MARY Ha!

SUSAN I hate to agree with the Spaniard, here, but—

      SIMON bites his lip.

MARY Half the country in her pocket, and I should put her in prison? Brilliant idea.

SUSAN Just until you've had a kid.

MARY I don't even have a boyfriend!

SUSAN Then get on that—

MARY *(close to the end of her wick)* Sometimes / you—

SUSAN —so that Bess is not your heir.
You don't want to be forced to deal with Bess, right? Then have a kid so she's not a threat.

MARY Who's running this joint?

SUSAN You are. Of / course.

MARY Thank you, Susan. Then I'll do things my way.

      SIMON makes a circle around this unresolved item on his agenda and stands waiting.

Hello. Simon. Something else?

SIMON takes a file and opens it on the table.

SIMON The question of your marriage, Majesty.

SUSAN Finally.

MARY Right. Done for the day, then.

MARY closes the file.

SUSAN What?

MARY I've had enough.

SUSAN How are you gonna have a kid if we don't talk about the husband?

MARY Done. We done?

MARY picks up the file and shoves it into SIMON's chest.

Yup. We're done. Now get out. All of you.

She picks up the sketches and gives them to SUSAN.

Like fifty pounds of clothes.

BASSETT Thirty-seven.

MARY It's time for the queen to hoist the weight of this island onto her completely inadequate shoulders.

SUSAN *(admonishing her doubt)* Mousie . . .

MARY Get lost. Go. Gwahn.

SIMON, BASSETT, and SUSAN leave.

Then there is silence. A strange silence.

MOTHERS

In between. MARY *turns to* CATALINA, *then turns to go.*
CATALINA *is not amused.*

CATALINA   You have been hiding something from me.

MARY   How can I hide something from you when you're a figment of my imagination? One might ask. Casually.

CATALINA   Are you ashamed?

MARY   Constantly. Of anything in particular?

CATALINA   You take her side. The daughter of the great whore.

MARY   A lot of water under that there bridge, Ma. And I don't have to like Bess to take responsibility for her.

CATALINA   She waits for you to fail.

MARY   *(ignoring that)* Also, we share a father. And five mothers. You—
(lifting her finger) You know what? I'm not dealing with this right now.

CATALINA   Your true retribution waits for Elizabeth.

MARY   And if your "true retribution" happened to walk around the corner, how easily do you think you'd take *her* on?

CATALINA   Time has given you power over that little bastard girl.

MARY   And it's all about power with you, ain't it.

    MARY does her best to retreat.

I'm about to be crowned the first reigning queen of England, okay? Me.

CATALINA   Mortifying, when she was born, what Henry did to you—

MARY   Bess will be there. At my side.

CATALINA	Denied you. Stripped you of your birth—
MARY	Can you think about me for just a second?
CATALINA	Couldn't face you, even—
MARY	Guess not.
CATALINA	Couldn't look you in the eye and tell you he was giving everything you were born to be . . . to her.
MARY	Yup.
CATALINA	Punishing *you* for *his* sins.
MARY	Okay, you wanna deal with the whore? Here you go. Deal with the whore.

Another figure, holding something in her arms, surreptitiously appears in the shadows.

MARY	Just hurry up and say what you need to say so that I can get on with my day, please.

ANNE steps forward from the shadows with the baby. CATALINA is immobilized.

CATALINA	Dios dame forza: did you bring her? *[God give me strength.]*
MARY	Yeah. Beat her up if you like. Talk to her about her kid. Go on, do it your way. Talk to her about what she and Henry put me through because you provoked them for eleven years.
CATALINA	How dare / you—
ANNE	Hold her.

ANNE gives the baby to MARY. MARY looks at the baby.

CATALINA	Bastarda.
ANNE	You'll have to get used to it.

CATALINA spits on the baby.

MARY   / Nice.

CATALINA   *(to ANNE)* Puta!

> *MARY carefully cleans the baby up with the tail of the blanket.*

ANNE   *(languidly, to CATALINA)* And you took such a high road once. When you thought I was just another mistress. When you thought he'd get tired of me, and I'd come crawling back to your circle of simpletons and be your partner at cards. Hmhmm. You were so wrong.
Elizabeth is no bastard. Elizabeth is a love child.

CATALINA   You hypnotized my husband. You forced him to banish me, to disown my Maria.

ANNE   You must think I am some hot shit to have that kind of control over the most powerful man in the world.

CATALINA   He was under your spell.

ANNE   Ohhhhhh, so I'm gifted with some sort of magical-sexual persuasion, is that it?
That's a myth, honey, there's no magic here. Just a little makeup and some great clothes.
I have a vagina. You have a vagina. If you think mine had any power over Henry that yours didn't, you don't know Henry.

CATALINA   You disgust me.

ANNE   I don't mind.

MARY   *(to the baby)* Three horrible people, weren't they? Not one of them cared about us.

CATALINA   For twenty-three years I was Henry's *true wife*. And now I have the final triumph. All that you did—all that you were responsible for—it doesn't matter now.
My daughter is Queen.

MARY	So that did register!
ANNE	In title only.
CATALINA	What else is there but the title?
ANNE	I didn't come to answer your rhetorical questions—
MARY	*(to ANNE)* Just a second, here: Who said you get a will of your own?
ANNE	—I came to put my child in your hands, sweet Mary. Look at her. You know what she is. You've known it all along. You know it every time she's standing in front of you. My daughter . . . is the *true queen.*
MARY	If she is ever Queen it'll have nothing to do with you. It'll have nothing to do with Henry. If she's a queen, it'll be because of the maddening little individual she has figured out how to be.
ANNE	My. Daughter.
MARY	Like you own her.
CATALINA	There. You are a covetous mother as well as a whore.
MARY	*(to CATALINA)* Hey! I'm not the fulfillment of your genetic expectations, either, get it?
CATALINA	Maria—!
MARY	Let us be. Just. Let us figure it out on our own.
CATALINA	I lived my entire life for this moment.
MARY	Then I'm sorry for you.
ANNE	I lived for fun. And Lizzie will too.
MARY	She calls herself Bess. And she's already had far too much fun, thank you very much. Along with her fair share of abandonment, incarceration, and public shaming.
ANNE	At least she's enjoyed some sexual abandon.

CATALINA   *Whore.*

ANNE   Actually, I didn't need to fuck him to bring him pleasure. Sorry if you did.

MARY   *(cooing with the baby)* Nice mommies. What hope do either of us have?

ANNE goes.

ANNE   *(to MARY)* Mind her head.

CATALINA   *(after her) My* daughter! *Queen*!

ANNE   *(casually, over her shoulder)* For how long?!

MARY chucks the baby under the chin.

MARY   I won't call you princess, 'kay? That's my line in the sand.

The baby starts to cry. MARY looks at her.

(a little too loudly) Quiet.

CATALINA comes to MARY and looks over her shoulder at the baby.

CATALINA   Kill her. Now.

MARY   *(are you nuts)* She's a *baby*.

CATALINA   She was never innocent. Think about what was done to you!

MARY   I *have*! I certainly did then.

CATALINA   You have the authority!

MARY   I sure do.

CATALINA   Queens can right the unbearable wrongs!

MARY   Queens can carry the burden of those wrongs. Even forgive them.
(to the baby) It's a challenge, but we can try.

CATALINA   And if the tables were turned? Do you think she would care for you? Ha!
That bastard would wring the life right out of you.
She would not think twice.

CORONATION

In public. MARY and BESS are on a balcony overlooking crowds of people. BESS stands slightly behind and to the right of MARY.

BESS   You can see for miles. The top of the Tower, that way. Look! Deer in the park!

MARY   I'm baking.

BESS   You look beautiful in purple.

MARY   I look old and tired.

BESS   *(yes)* No.

    A moment.

MARY   What was that about, you know, when you joined me riding into the city?

BESS   Showing support. For your claim.

MARY   You came with a lot of folks. In such bright new outfits.

BESS   The people need to see that the bastards have resources.

MARY   A thousand horsemen. Rather intimidating resources.

BESS   I was making your case.

    MARY gives BESS a look.

Can't you let me do anything for you?

    MARY continues to look at BESS sideways.

I am your obedient subject and humble sister.

MARY   What did you do with the real Bess?

BESS   Wave.

MARY   Right.

They wave.

BESS   So. You decided to cave.

MARY   I . . . did what?

BESS   The prisoners: Edward Courtenay, Henry Grey; you set them free.

MARY   That's what I was supposed to do.

BESS   I . . . I just question the shrewdness of that policy.

MARY   It's not a policy, it's a *tradition.*
(demonstrating) You take some non-threatening prisoners from the overthrow—*(à la John Wayne)* "These are my prisoners," all manly like—and then, poof, you set them free. It's a . . . custom.

BESS   *(still skeptical)* It's . . . old-fashioned.

MARY   *(beginning to doubt)* Shows people what a shiny new ruler they have. Starts things off on the right foot.

BESS   As long as . . .

MARY   What?!

BESS   You deal with the challengers as well.

MARY   Gosh. I'm so grateful you told me that.

BESS   You're welcome. Father had to do it all the time. The closer the challenger, the more important to show dominance.

MARY (*considering who's standing next to her*) I'll bear that in mind. There are plenty of reasons to obliterate the opposition, you know. What I'm trying to demonstrate are the reasons to tolerate it.

>   *BESS gives MARY a tolerant smile.*

(*her, too*) Go on, then: weigh in on Jane!

BESS (*finally!*) She sat on *your throne*. For nine whole days.

MARY Yup, and? What would you do?

BESS Execute her.

MARY Just like that.

BESS She's annoying. And she's ambitious.

MARY Pot. Black.

BESS I would have torn off that bandage as soon as I got to London. You've let sentiment get in your way.

MARY Yeah. I have. She comes from a pair of fucked-up parents who completely ruined her childhood with their own greedy little ambitions; her only solace from those parents, and her *siblings*, who grew more and more *untrustworthy*, was her faith—her devotion to *God*.
How could I begin to have empathy.

BESS Jane wants your job.

MARY Jane wants to go back to dancing on her father's feet and being his little princess.

BESS She was never a princess. And when you decided to seize her crown, your days of being a princess were over. You are a *queen*. Your pretty little cousin sat on your throne. You are the only thing standing in the way of her doing it again.

MARY   Oh, I have a crazy feeling *you'd* stand in her way, too. You'd raise a rebellion if you thought for a second that she was heading for my chair ahead of you.

(finishing the conversation) I won't just let her walk, but I will not have her killed.

BESS   *(sweetly, giving in)* Okay.

MARY   Really?

BESS   *(not really)* You are going to be an amazing queen.

> MARY *looks at* BESS.

Wave.

MARY   Oh.

> *They both smile and wave for a moment.*

BESS   I think you talk now.

MARY   I hate this part.

> MARY *moves to the front of the balcony to address the public.*

(a bit too angry and a bit too loud) The voice of the purple— The voice of the *people* is the voice of God . . . by who's goodness I am now settled in just possession of the imperial crown of this our realm.

(making her points to BESS *as well as the crowd)* I have delivered swift *justice* to those who stood against me in my rightful accession, and have shown due *clemency* to the innocent and the unjustly imprisoned.

I cannot and will not now hide that religion which God and the world knows I have professed since my infancy, and I would be glad if all of you quietly and charitably embraced the old religion, the tradition upon which our nationhood stands, the same tradition that my father Henry held deeply in his heart.

Still . . . I wish to make clear, that it is not in my mind to *compel* any of you to make that choice, until such time as your common assent is achieved by an act of parliament.

For now, I ask you to live side by side with each other's beliefs, in God given grace and charity.

> *BESS steps forward, raises MARY's hand with hers, and leads a cheer.*

BESS God save and protect Mary the Queen!

CLEMENCY

> *In private. JANE is in a prison cell. MARY is with her.*

JANE I'm not like Bess. I never wanted this.
I never asked for it, Mary. You believe that, don't you?

MARY Bess would say the same thing. Why not accept a little responsibility.

JANE I would never have even imagined taking the—no, not that I was *taking* the crown: I wasn't even reaching for it, I— Oh my, listen to me prattling on: I don't want to die for something I didn't do.

MARY You're not going to die.

JANE Then let me out of here.

MARY I can't. Not just yet. There's . . . pressure to . . .

JANE What?

MARY Kill the girl.

JANE No.

MARY / I can't—

JANE I didn't—

MARY *(deferring)* After you, little Jane Grey, as you seem to have a fondness for going before me.

JANE I didn't know anything about this until three days before Eddie died and the crown was being fitted for my head.

MARY Then you're not as smart as everyone reports you to be.

JANE I pray to God every day that you'll forgive me.

MARY Yeah, see, asking forgiveness implies you've done something wrong.

    This error lands on JANE.

JANE I don't know how to behave around you anymore, Mary. It's all happening so fast. My head's spinning.

MARY At least it's still attached.

JANE Oh God.

MARY Kidding, totally kidding. My head's spinning too.
Simon says if I destroy the entire Grey household they'll never regroup to take my crown.

JANE Don't listen to Simon.

MARY Simon says, "Power and tyranny have more place in the affairs of state than right or justice."

JANE Do you think that's true?

MARY Do you think it's true?

JANE I don't want it to be true. Not in this moment.

MARY I want to do the right thing.

JANE That's what I want too.

MARY You're so . . . honest.

    A moment.

Aren't you?

A moment.

Why didn't you run? You could have run!

JANE From the king? I was doing what he told me.

MARY Eddie didn't tell you anything: he was barfing blood that whole month. You had to know something was up when Dudley married you to his son!

JANE *(believe me)* I didn't want to marry Guildford Dudley! I was pushed. By his father. By mine.

MARY Or you jumped.

JANE I was doing what I was told.

MARY Why? Did Dudley torture you?

JANE No.

MARY Did your father threaten your life?

JANE Not exactly.

MARY Then?
Never bargain away your cherry.

JANE If all you know is how to please the man in charge, then you please the man in charge.

MARY Ah. And you think we have that in common.

JANE We do.

MARY Unh-uh, see, I stood up to my father. I fought him for years, not days. I took *responsibility* for what I believed was right and just. Even under duress.

JANE And where did that get you?

MARY Are you judging me?

JANE Henry was brutal to you!

MARY	He was.
JANE	I can't face my father's brutality. I don't have your courage. *(on a tangent)* What happens to a girl who has no courage?
MARY	*(the stroke of the axe)* Whmff. *(the head falling)* Gnk. Gnk. Gnk.
JANE	That's not funny.
MARY	Meh? Maybe a little bit funny.
JANE	*(back on track)* I don't have your agency.
MARY	Don't you want it?
JANE	Do you?

MARY says nothing.

I'm a disciple. A witness. That's my way.

MARY	Follow the leader, play along with everything they say, and, hey presto! you're Queen of England.
JANE	No.
MARY	Maybe.
JANE	No!
MARY	Come on. You wanted it. Everybody wants it: me, Bess, you. We just have different ways of getting it.

JANE stops and thinks.

JANE	Is that possible? That by following the rules I did the wrong thing?

JANE thinks again.

I must have wanted it. One tiny bit.

MARY	That's good to hear. That's realistic.
JANE	So you'll kill me now. Because I *am* responsible.
MARY	I'm okay with that.

JANE	You are?
MARY	If people are straight with me? I'm all good. It's when people try to get what they want through . . .
JANE	Deception.
MARY	Guile. Treachery. *Mendacity*. My father hated that. That's when he pushed back.
JANE	Boy. Bess must be shaking in her boots.

MARY considers this. She prepares to go.

MARY	I'm leaving you in the Tower. It'll protect you from the lunatics as much as it protects me.
JANE	For how long?
MARY	Let things settle. Let my parliament implement some of its policy. Then we'll revisit this.
JANE	Thanks, Mary.

A moment.

MARY	It makes me look weak.
JANE	Keeping me alive?
MARY	You're not the only one judging me.
JANE	God is our only judge.

MARY turns to go.

MARY	Oh. *(casually dropping a bomb)* We should talk about your conversion.
JANE	My . . . conversion?
MARY	Next visit. *(and . . . onward)* It is absolutely my intention to pardon you, Jane Grey, and soon after that to release you.

JANE runs and throws her arms around MARY.

JANE   I'm so grateful you trust me.

    MARY stiffens and manages a tight smile.

MARY   Gee whiz.

INTERNATIONAL TRADE DEAL

    At table. SIMON stands with a file. SUSAN and BASSETT
    sit at the table with a chart. MARY looks out the window.

MARY   *(steamed)* Who I choose to marry is none of their goddamn business!

BASSETT   Well, it is / actually.

MARY   Do they choose for *kings*?

BASSETT   No, but / you—

MARY   See!

SUSAN   We all want you to have a kid; the Council is just more vocal / in their—

MARY   You think Henry would allow the *Council* to choose his *wives*? I'd like to see that happen.
    (to SIMON) I'd like to see what he'd do to anyone who would advise it.

SIMON   Merely the messenger, Your Majesty.

MARY   Did Beatrice have to get permission to marry Ben?

SIMON   Beatrice?
    (to SUSAN) Who's / Beatrice?

SUSAN   The laundress. Married the horse guy.

MARY	Did anyone even *suggest* that she marry Geoffrey from over in kitchens? No! A *laundress* can choose her own husband, but a *queen* can't.
BASSETT	The queen's consort is a tad more important than the horse guy.
SIMON	The Council want you to *consider* him.
MARY	Edward bloody Courtenay.
BASSETT	He's a good Catholic.
SUSAN	And he likes you!
MARY	Of course he does: I gave him a "get out of jail free" card.
SUSAN	You owe him at least a look.
MARY	I *owe* him?!
SUSAN	There *is* no one else, Mouse.
BASSETT	He's the only peer of yours left.
MARY	And he's a totally decent guy, but. Edward Courtenay's been in prison half his life, and . . .
SUSAN	What?
MARY	I'd have to have sex with him! That's what.
SUSAN	Ohhh—
MARY	He doesn't even know which fork to use for fish.
SUSAN	He can be taught.
MARY	I'm thirty-eight. I haven't got time for us both to figure out what goes where.
SIMON	There is great peril in leaving your sister as heir.
MARY	No shit.
SUSAN	*(terrible thought)* Or the other Mary.

BASSETT	You know that's exactly what the French are hoping: that you'll die childless and let them slip across the channel with Mary Stuart.
SIMON	Will you *consider* Edward Courtenay?
MARY	I will *not*. I will *consider* having a child, because—you wanna know why, Simon?
SIMON	Yes, Your Majesty.
MARY	Because it would get you off my back about killing Jane and throwing Bess in a dungeon.
SIMON	I'm afraid having a single heir of your body will not provide the necessary security to divert that course.

SUSAN looks at the picture of Courtenay.

SUSAN	*(optimistically)* He's not bad looking.
MARY	A super nice guy. *(read my lips)* I Will Not Marry Edward Courtenay. He's already suffered enough.
SIMON	Then. We must look to Europe.
SUSAN	Oh, dear, no: the Council won't agree to that. The country won't agree to it.
MARY	*You* won't agree to it.
SUSAN	I've never liked foreigners.
MARY	My mother was a foreigner. And what choice do we have?
SUSAN	The English don't trust Europeans.
SIMON	The feeling is reciprocal, I might add.
MARY	We can't wait around for Bess to get even more attractive. *(to SIMON)* What are my prospects in Europe?
SUSAN	Don't even look!

MARY	Then maybe *you'd* like to get naked with Edward Courtenay.
BASSETT	Imagine.
SIMON	*(a small explosion)* We are conducting business in this room, not women's chit-chat!
MARY	Easy there, Simon. If it was up to me, I wouldn't marry at all. I've seen enough of what happens in marriage to last me a lifetime, thank you very much.
BASSETT	Public duty.
MARY	I know.
BASSETT	Security for the kingdom.
MARY	Yup.
SUSAN	Marriage can be fun sometimes, too, you know.
MARY	Blah, blah, blah.
SIMON	We've had interest from Portugal.
MARY	*(cringing)* Inbred. Creepy.
BASSETT	I have a thing for Dutch men. *Nothing.* Germans? *Nothing.* The French are out.
SIMON	Spain is looking to secure a sea route to the Netherlands.
MARY	And we just happen to have one without a ring on her finger.
SIMON	We have had an official proposal from your cousin, the Holy Roman Emperor Charles V, on behalf of his son, Philip.

The room goes quiet. SIMON *places a picture of Philip on the table and moves it toward* MARY. MARY *turns the picture face down without looking at it. She holds her belly.*

MARY   What happened to cousin Phil's engagement to the Portuguese girl?

SIMON   As far as we know that arrangement is not final.

SUSAN   As far as you know?

SIMON   *(to MARY)* If the emperor is willing to engage in negotiations, Your Majesty should be willing to reciprocate.

A silence.

MARY   You can tell the emperor that his son is a greater match than I could possibly deserve.

SIMON   I will convey your pleasure. And encourage provision of their terms.

SUSAN   The English won't play along that easily.

MARY   *Who* won't play along?

SUSAN   *(scolding)* Don't you take me for granted, young lady.

MARY   Oh, trust me . . .
Hey, Simon: how do Chuck and Phil see us selling a Spanish engagement to the folks here at home?

SIMON   They feel that the Council and the people *(looks at SUSAN)* will easily see the political and economic benefits of an alliance with Spain, including the profit and influence that will be attainable in Europe for the offspring of your union.

MARY   Free trade for the people. European passports for the kids.

BASSETT   For your *legitimate* heirs.

MARY   That's the long game, right?

SIMON   The Empire is just as concerned as you are about Elizabeth's ascendancy.

MARY   Yup. I should have a baby.

SIMON   He will be King of England and France, Naples, Jerusalem, and Ireland; Defender of the Faith; Prince of Spain and Sicily; Archduke of Austria; Duke of Milan, Burgundy, and Brabant; Count of Habsburg, Flanders, and Tyrol.

MARY   King, Prince, Duke, Count—
(to BASSETT) Maybe we can slip a little gender parity clause into the pre-nup for the daughters.

SIMON   I have no doubt you will bear this country a healthy son.

MARY   Well, I have enough doubt for both of us. I'm a virgin, you see, Simon. Kind of an old virgin.
So how badly does Spain want that safe sea passage to the Netherlands?

SIMON   That will become clear when I convey your interest and availability, along with a flattering portrait.

MARY   Good luck with that.

SUSAN   *(scolding)* Mouse.

SIMON   Will that be all, Your Majesty?

MARY   Sure. Thanks Simon.

SIMON   *(with a deep diplomatic bow)* My duty and pleasure, Your Majesty.

> SIMON *goes.* MARY *picks up the picture of Philip and looks at it. She bursts into tears.*

SUSAN   Mousie . . .

MARY   He's so cute. Look.

SUSAN   He's pretty cute.

MARY	He's too good-looking for me.
SUSAN	What a thing to say.
MARY	So much younger.
BASSETT	Only eleven years.
MARY	*(salt / wound)* See! He doesn't want to be with me.
SUSAN	You don't know that.
MARY	Eighteen engagements. None of them wanted me. They were only interested in . . .
BASSETT	The booty.
MARY	Bassett knows: she's had her day in the bargain bin.
SUSAN	You undersell yourself.
MARY	Because I'm not meant to be *sold*! I'm not a commodity! And now I'm supposed to trust this . . . *(looking at the picture)* too young, fucking gorgeous skirt chaser! Trust him with my life *and* the booty. How do I do that? I don't know how to do that. How do I trust the second in command of a multinational arms consortium when I can't even trust my own family?

CUSTODY BATTLE

In between. MARY *and* CATALINA.

CATALINA	Of course you can trust me. It's your father you can't trust: he always lied to you.
MARY	*(finding courage)* You lied. I think you lied.
CATALINA	What are you talking about.

MARY	You lied to everyone. Didn't you.
CATALINA	Lied about what?
MARY	About being a virgin when you married / Henry.
CATALINA	Maria! Don't you dare to question me on this / matter.
MARY	You and Arthur were a couple of teenaged kids, / Ma.
CATALINA	Don't you / dare.
MARY	He arrived in his nightgown and stayed all night in your room!
CATALINA	We prayed.
MARY	You can't possibly / think— [people believe that.]
CATALINA	That first marriage didn't matter in the end: the bed I shared with your father was sanctified by the pope.
MARY	Ha! Lying is okay, then, as long as you get the pope on side.
CATALINA	A mother will do anything for her child. Anything. That is why we commodify ourselves. Don't speak to me as if you are above it. What are you negotiating with Philip? What will your body buy?
MARY	I'm hammering out a future for my children, not leaving them to fend for themselves!
CATALINA	I was *forced* to leave you.
MARY	I don't buy that for a nickel: all the Catholics in Europe were on our side. You coulda nailed Henry! But did you call the forces to our aid? / No.
CATALINA	No, I—
MARY	You sat, alone, in the cold, in the middle of the Fens. What was that about?!
CATALINA	Strategy.

MARY He imprisons you in a castle in the middle of nowhere, keeps you from *seeing* your only daughter—

CATALINA I had / no—

MARY —from *writing* your only daughter . . . and you . . . just . . . go along with it?

CATALINA I / didn't—

MARY What kind of strategy is that?

CATALINA I was killing him with kindness.

MARY *(no)* You couldn't stand up to him; you were so desperate to uphold the mythical love story you'd invented, if he told you to go jump in the lake around Kimbolton Castle you would have done it. *(scoffing)* The "true wife"—

CATALINA I was protecting you—

MARY Bullshit! You abandoned me!

CATALINA Never—

MARY And your obstinacy made him hate me.

CATALINA He wanted to take you from me.

MARY No, see, he said exactly the opposite.

CATALINA How could he—?

MARY "Choose your mother"—that's what he told me. "Hate me, write me off, whatever you have to do. I'm getting a divorce. I'm starting another family." Like I should just look the other way while he ditched everything I knew to go have sex with a porn star.
(you two) Nice parents. *(me)* Piggy in the middle.

CATALINA He saw your power.

MARY He *took* any power I might have had because of *you*.

CATALINA The power of your blood.

MARY   Will you stop already with the / blood?!

CATALINA   You are refusing to hear / me!

MARY   I don't *want* to hear you!
You split me in half. Just like you split the country.
You know where that left me?

> *MARY leaves CATALINA hanging. Then drops her.*

Holding on to Bess.

> *If CATALINA is stung by this, she barely shows it. She deliberately plays a card.*

CATALINA   Your father began to draft legislation for my execution.

MARY   *(shocked)* Shut up, shut up, he never did.

CATALINA   Your father was a cold-blooded killer. He wanted me dead.

MARY   No. No way. You didn't know him at the end. He wasn't a bad guy. Just. Stuck.

CATALINA   He was heading to parliament. To be rid of me, / Maria—

MARY   Not true, / not true—

CATALINA   And you were next.

MARY   I can't— I don't even know how to hear that.

CATALINA   Henry.

MARY   Was gonna kill me.

CATALINA   His heir.

> *A moment.*

His *heir*.

> *A moment.*

MARY   Ooohh, you are a sly one, Doña Catalina d'Aragón.

'Cause I just happen to have a couple of *heirs* hanging about that are a bit of a pain in the ass, so you think I should draft legislation to kill *them*! Like father, like daughter: is that it?

CATALINA   There are unfortunate inevitabilities one has to confront in order to maintain one's office.
Henry knew: he could trust no one.
Least of all the first in line to the throne.

CHRISTMAS PRESENT

At table. MARY *sits at the seat of power. She is anxious and not well. To her right is a gift box.* BESS *enters.*

BESS   Your Majesty.

MARY   Shut up.

BESS   I respect you. I want to show it.

MARY   Siddown.

A moment. The sisters assess each other.

BESS   How are things with Philip?

MARY   He sent a proxy to our engagement party.

BESS   Oh. Darn.

MARY   And his father sent me a present.

MARY shows BESS *the pendant brooch.*

Sorta hoped he'd do the shopping / himself.

BESS   Oooo, a pearl. A really *big* pearl.

A long silence while MARY *continues to look at* BESS. BESS *feels this.*

MARY   Do *you* trust *me*?

BESS   With what?

MARY   Talk to me. About the rift. Between us.

BESS   *(a little too defensive)* What have you found out?

MARY   Good Lord: what are you hiding?!

An impasse.

BESS   *(the rift)* Okay. Like. Politically?

MARY   Let's start with religion.

BESS   Well . . . I don't see us as being that divided. I mean, I come to mass with you every day.

MARY   Do you keep your fingers crossed?

BESS   What do you mean by that?

A moment.

MARY   Where do you think God is?

BESS   In England?

MARY   If God was a part of your body, what part would God be?

BESS   I think . . . my mind.
Well . . . ?
Is there a right answer?

MARY   No.

BESS   My mind, then. Where do you think?

MARY   My heart.

BESS   Oh.
Both, right?

MARY   The heart is more sentimental than the mind. More emotional. More . . . out of control.

BESS   I never thought of it that way.

MARY	You don't believe in the old traditions, do you?
BESS	These questions are weird.
MARY	Don't! equivocate!
BESS	Okay! Why do you want to know?
MARY	Because . . . it's the only way out.
BESS	Of what.
MARY	If you believe one thing, and I believe another thing, one of us has to change what they believe: one of us has to convert.
BESS	Or what?
MARY	Or you and I will never have peace. Our country will never integrate again.

BESS looks at MARY without giving anything away.

Simon says I should worry about you.

BESS	Oh, I'm all right. I had that little cold last week, that's all—
MARY	Bess. *Worry* about you.
BESS	Oh. Like that kind of worry.
MARY	My engagement to Spain has pissed off the French.
BESS	You had to know that would happen.
MARY	The French are pushing me to marry / Edward—
BESS	Edward Courtenay.
MARY	Uhuh. It would be an . . . *impressive strategy*, don't you think? One that you might choose.
BESS	He *is* the great-grandson of a king.
MARY	You like him, don't you.
BESS	I think he's cute.
MARY	I've heard.

BESS   What?

MARY   That the French are backing a plan to put you and Courtenay on the throne.

BESS   Together?

MARY   Married.

BESS   On your throne?

MARY   That's the one.

BESS   You know how I feel about rumours.

MARY   I've taken action against him.

BESS   Oh?

MARY   Courtenay's in custody.

BESS   Oh. Is he.

MARY   We're questioning him now.

BESS   What do you think he'll say?

MARY   Everything. I don't suppose he wants another fifteen years in the Tower.

BESS   I don't suppose.

MARY   What do you think he'll say about you?

BESS   There's nothing *to* say.

MARY   Off the record.

BESS   I don't speak off the record. You taught me that.

MARY   I did. Which only complicates the picture.

BESS   How?

MARY   I can't trust you!

BESS   That's not / fair.

MARY   You've done it before, Bess! With Thom? To Eddie?

(asking the question) Are you going to marry Edward Courtenay and try to take the throne from / me?

BESS   You'd rather I was married off to some lonely European three times my age and sent to Lower / Slobbovia!

MARY   Oh, for Pete's sake: answer me honestly for / once!

BESS   *(answering honestly)* Okay. Your ideas are ridiculous: you can't put the country in reverse; it won't work.
I'm just being prudent. You give me no / choice.

MARY   Don't do this. Don't do this. God, you are just like your moth/er.

BESS   I am / not!!

MARY   You look just like her. You're about the same age now as she was / when— [Anne came on the scene with Henry].

BESS   I can't help looking like my / mother.

MARY   Forgive me for all the hatred you stir in my / heart.

BESS   Hate me! Go on then! Hate / me!

MARY   I want you to go. Go.

BESS   No.

MARY   GO! So I / don't—

BESS   I can believe what you believe. I can believe anything.

MARY   See, your *heart* can't possibly do that. It would just be changing your *mind*.

BESS   Don't send me away, Mary. Don't. Don't send me / away!

MARY   You'll do anything to get what you / want!

BESS   I can't help being more determined than you. I was born this way. I can't help being the talented sister.

MARY reels.

MARY   You'll kill me, won't you. You won't even / blink.

BESS   Don't ask those / questions.

MARY   Jesus. I have helped / you!

BESS   You promised Father.

MARY   And what? Oh, I get it. That's why *you* promise nothing. That's why you are faithful to no one. That's why you have no religion: you make no choices; you sit on the fence, because / then—

BESS   Then no one gets hurt.

MARY   I am *someone*! If you kill me it will hurt!

BESS   Never. I would never do that, Mary. You have to believe me.

MARY   But if I just happen to die as a result of one of your plots, then . . .

BESS   We are after the same thing.

MARY   NO!

BESS   Yes. And you don't have what it takes. You may have inherited the right to rule, but you simply don't have the talent.

MARY   It doesn't take TALENT to draft legislation and have you killed!

BESS   Do it then. Don't just threaten it! Let's see you do / it!

MARY   Damn / you!

BESS   No, damn you!

MARY   One of us will be damned. It's inevitable. One of us will be damned by the other's indoctrination. Because there is a chasm between us that will never be bridged. Because I can't trust you. And you won't trust me.

An impasse.

BESS   I'm sorry, Mary.

MARY	For what.
BESS	For being the one who'll win.
MARY	Fuck you.

MARY makes up her mind to proceed.

Here.

MARY hands BESS the gift box.

I was saving it for Christmas.

BESS	Don't send me away. I don't have anyone anymore.
MARY	Just! Take it! Take it with you. Put it in your stocking at Hatfield.
BESS	You think you can hurt me?
MARY	Go!
BESS	No!

Another impasse.

I can hurt you more. You have to kill Jane Grey!

MARY	I don't. I don't.
BESS	She'll never convert. Her faith is in her heart. Just like yours. You have to kill that sentimental heart. You have no choice!

BESS opens the box and takes out a small silver crucifix. She looks at it. Looks at MARY. She makes the sign of the cross, then kisses the crucifix.

End of Act One.

ACT TWO
ANOTHER VIRGIN TRIAL

In private. JANE is in a prison cell. She has just come from her trial and is wearing a black dress with jet buttons. MARY, who is tired and agitated, is with her.

MARY   I didn't fight for a trial for you so that you could walk into the courtroom and then, two minutes later, walk out!

JANE   I *did* take possession of the Tower; I *was* proclaimed queen. I couldn't exactly say those things didn't happen.

MARY   Can't you be just a little bit disagreeable? You were meant to rat out the bullies.

JANE   The Council had already made up their minds.

MARY   So the decision's back on my plate!

JANE   That's what's best, isn't it? You're going to grant me a reprieve.

MARY   We'll talk about that.

JANE   *(now)* Okay.

MARY   It pushes my buttons, you see, when people harp on about their goodness. Tout it, even. My sister does that. Every time she backs herself into a corner. I don't trust her. That's—no: *can't* trust her. Can't trust anyone.

JANE   I accepted responsibility. That's what you wanted, isn't it?

MARY considers this.

MARY   Okay: Guildford asked you if he might be crowned King when you became Queen . . . and you said no.

JANE   He has no right.

MARY   *(but you do?)* Yeah, so, I find it hard to reconcile how you didn't want to be Queen at all, but then when Guildford offered to . . . share the burden, you were like, nope: thanks, the job's all mine. That seems, well, not so much like the humble little Lutheran, if you know what I mean. That maybe you'd given a thought or two to the political ramifications of a decision like that.

JANE   Guildford and me, we're like you and Philip.

MARY   *(raising an eyebrow)* Wow. Are you.

JANE   Sure. When a man joins up, he has an expectation that the woman will just step aside to have babies. I wanted to be clear, as I think you do: *you* are the ruling monarch; Philip will be your *consort.*
Right?
That's how I intended things to go with Guildford: he would be my consort.

MARY is uncomfortable with JANE's use of titles.

MARY   So alike, aren't we.

JANE   Guildford doesn't have royal blood.

MARY   But you do.

JANE   And Guildford wasn't named by the king.

MARY   But you were.

JANE   Yes. To both of those things. I can't pretend they're not true.

MARY   I don't know, you seem like a pretty good pretender to me. *(the second point)* You lived with Katherine Parr and Thomas Seymour at Chelsea after my father died.

JANE   You know I did.

MARY   Did you learn a lot?

JANE   Kate taught me Plutarch. And medicine. And Thomas, well . . . he had a very generous spirit.

MARY   I know all about his generosity.
        Kate though . . . she had . . . ambitions . . . to be a queen, and all: Did she talk to you about those?

JANE   She did.

MARY   Queen school.

JANE   *(amused)* That's exactly what it was!

MARY   There! And Thom was trying to get you married to my brother; to the *king* . . .

JANE   Yes, but Eddie wasn't interested.

MARY   You're missing my point.

JANE   Oh, sorry. Your point.

MARY   You meet all the requirements, you see—breeding, cultivation, education—and those negotiations between Thom and Eddie . . . that was your window. What was your expectation?

JANE   As soon as that window closed, any expectation was gone. Completely. I have no proof of that, but I'm asking you to believe me.

MARY   Cross your heart?

JANE   *(slightly shocked)* I don't do that.

MARY wrinkles her nose.

MARY   If I could see inside your heart, what would I see?

JANE   I don't understand the question.

MARY   *(impatient)* Just— [take a stab].

        JANE considers this.

JANE   Truth.

MARY   *(a little surprised)* Not faith?

JANE   Faith is truth.

MARY   Uhuh. Yours is a very different truth than mine.
        If you had to, could you change that truth?

JANE   Truth is truth. There is no changing it.

        MARY is reminded of someone from her past.

MARY   Do you know who John Fisher was?

JANE   He was a treasonous heretic. Your father had him executed.

MARY   Do you think that decision was just?

JANE   John Fisher was a sacrilegious heathen.

MARY   No equivocation there.

        MARY starts to go.

JANE   Why do you keep coming to talk to me, Mary?

        MARY stops.

MARY   Look, I can arrange for you and your husband to see each
        other, if you want.

JANE   I never liked Guildford.

MARY   Suit yourself.

JANE   How much longer?

MARY	Philip should arrive within the next couple of months. Once I'm pregnant—that kind of security for the country—that should pave your way.
	Fingers crossed.
JANE	That's . . .
MARY	What.

JANE averts her eyes and says nothing.

What?

JANE	To make the sign of the cross with one's fingers in hopes of achieving one's will?
	Blasphemous.
MARY	Yup.

MARY goes.

FISHING

In between. MARY and CATALINA. MARY is preparing for bed.

CATALINA	You're procrastinating!
MARY	I'm trying to work it out, okay?!
	I'm trying to understand about Jane—no—well?—about me—about *Henry*, okay? How he was able to kill people—to have people killed.
	Something Jane said made me think about John Fisher.
CATALINA	Oh, John! He was my champion! He stood up to Henry with such unwavering courage. If only you had witnessed him arguing my case.
MARY	But they were friends. Good friends. How could Henry kill John Fisher?

CATALINA	Fisher stood in absolute defiance of Henry. He wouldn't accept the divorce.
MARY	Because of his faith?
CATALINA	Their friendship could survive a few religious disagreements. But when those disagreements became political disagreements? John wore down Henry's patience.
MARY	I totally get that: I'm losing patience with Jane. But to *kill*? I mean, if it's just politics . . . you know, you yell for a while, and then you pound the table, and when the bell rings, you go across the street for a pint.
CATALINA	The divorce changed everything for them.
MARY	How?
CATALINA	The divorce was a wedge that split the country. And at the moment of that splitting, a force that was equal and opposite irrevocably fused religion and politics. When Henry drove that wedge into the country, the religious foe—who might be forgiven, who might be disagreed with—became the political foe who must be alienated, who must be . . . / eliminated.
MARY	Eliminated.
CATALINA	Henry killed Fisher because Fisher was *right*.
MARY	Wait. No. Father didn't believe that.
CATALINA	*John Fisher* did. With pious conviction.
MARY	*(considering who she's speaking to)* And there's nothing the public love more than an altruistic martyr.
CATALINA	Yes. In that populism lies the danger: because even if the people know they have to obey your laws, they can see the power—they can see the *good*, the *right*—in an innocent young girl who won't.

MARY	What pushed Henry over the edge, then?
CATALINA	What is pushing you over the edge?
MARY	Her certainty. Her integrity.
CATALINA	Yes! Trust your instincts!
MARY	I don't want to!
CATALINA	Her righteousness is your enemy.
MARY	If I can't find the common ground between me and that little girl, how can I ask my country to look for it? I have to see her with an open heart.
CATALINA	The heart backs down. The heart is weak.
MARY	*(a seed is planted)* The heart is weak.
CATALINA	When someone aggressively tries to take something that is rightfully yours, you have no choice but to enforce your own law. Your own sense of order. What are you waiting for?
MARY	Certainty. At what point have I been diligent enough to proclaim the beliefs of a sixteen-year-old girl a threat to law and order?

A moment. MARY *gets into bed.*

CATALINA	It was predicted, you know.
MARY	What.
CATALINA	That at the beginning of Henry's reign he would be as gentle as a lamb, and by the end . . . more deadly than a lion.
MARY	He had a choice.
CATALINA	The predators were approaching. He chose to be what a king must be.

ACTION MOVIE 2—THE WYATT REBELLION

> *At bed.* MARY *is sleeping.* SUSAN *enters quickly with a lamp, followed by* BASSETT *with a briefing notebook.* SUSAN *gently shakes* MARY.

SUSAN Mousie. Mouse. / Quickly, pet. Get up.

MARY *(coming out of a dream)* A lion . . . hiding . . .

> MARY *catapults awake.*

Bess?

BASSETT Bess?

MARY Is she— I saw—
(to SUSAN*)* Is it Bess?

SUSAN Not Bess. Up. Simon's coming to brief you.

MARY About—?

BASSETT The French fleet are assembling off the Normandy coast.

> SUSAN *helps* MARY *to dress.*

MARY Why? What are / they—?

BASSETT They're backing a rebellion.

MARY Rebellion where?

SUSAN Here.

MARY Where here?

BASSETT A four-pronged attack against the city.

MARY Jesus.

SUSAN Courtenay let it slip.

MARY Courtenay. In the Tower.

SUSAN He gave us the heads-up.

MARY	It's Bess.
BASSETT	*(the good news)* Three points of the rebellion have already faltered: the leader of the Cornwall faction has fled to France; the Welshmen / never—
SUSAN	Never even got out of their beds—
BASSETT	And Henry Grey has been arrested in Leicestershire.
MARY	Henry Grey.
BASSETT	You should never have set him free at your coronation.
MARY	Thanks. Four points, you said. Who's left?
BASSETT	Thomas Wyatt.
MARY	*My* Thomas Wyatt? *Against* me? No way.
BASSETT	In Kent.
MARY	You're wrong. You've gotta be wrong. He was on my side against Dudley. I gave him a pretty silver medal!
SUSAN	He's on the march.
BASSETT	With the French assembling across the channel: keeping the Spaniards from taking our side.
MARY	That old trick.

SIMON *enters hastily. He averts his eyes.*

SIMON	Your Majesty.
MARY	Cut to the chase, Simon.
SIMON	The French—
MARY	The Normandy coast. Yes.
SIMON	They're taking action against your marriage with Spain.
MARY	I'm not marrying the entire country.
SUSAN	We better retreat.

BASSETT   We better *attack*.

MARY   *(that doesn't sound right)* Attack France?

BASSETT   Attack Wyatt.

SIMON   Immediate orders are needed to rally your loyal support.

MARY   *(it doesn't make sense)* Why would Wyatt raise a rebellion?

SUSAN   I have a notion.

BASSETT   What?

SUSAN   He has no love of Spain.

MARY   Nor do you, but you're not storming the castle.

SUSAN   When his father was a diplomat for your father—heading to Rome—Wyatt saw it first-hand. The Inquisition. The torture. The executions.

BASSETT   When he was a kid?

SUSAN   *(to SIMON)* Spanish atrocities.

SIMON   *(to SUSAN)* You women would have the world all milk and honey.

SUSAN   We *women* are incapable of that kind of horror.

SIMON   All humans are capable.

MARY   For heaven's sake, my marriage is a trade deal. I'm not putting out a welcome mat for Spain's radicals. I'll talk to Wyatt.

SUSAN   Oh no you don't. *We* are heading for the hills.

SIMON   The sovereign must lead but he must not fall.

> *MARY has no idea what to do. She looks from SUSAN to BASSETT.*

MARY   So, so, do I go, or do I stay?

> *SIMON sucks in his cheeks.*

SIMON	There is concern among the Council that the queen is relying too heavily on the advice of unqualified women.

A moment.

BASSETT	We need to muster troops.
SUSAN	We need to pack and leave.
MARY	*(grasping)* What about the London guard? Can we send them? They're armed and ready.
SUSAN	They're guarding *you*.

BASSETT writes down the order.

SIMON	Your / Majesty—
SUSAN	No way, Mousie. We can't leave you with/out—
SIMON	Sending the London guard would leave you vulnerable / to a—
MARY	We'll replace them as soon we can assemble another detail, but they can go right now, can't they?
BASSETT	Armed and ready.
MARY	Faster than trying to pull a new force together in the middle of the night.

SIMON, SUSAN, and BASSETT are caught in a conflict of protocol.

	Hello? Anyone?
BASSETT	Faster. Yes.
MARY	Then do it. Hey, and send a negotiator.
SIMON	This is no time for negotiation, Your / Majesty—
MARY	Words, Simon. Our first weapons. Give the rebels every chance to surrender before the guns come out.

SIMON   It is not / wise—

MARY   I thought you had no opinion, Simon.

    BASSETT hands SIMON *the order.* SIMON *turns to go.*

And Simon.

SIMON   Majesty.

MARY   I have the right to choose my own husband, from Spain or from Shropshire. Every single soldier that fights for me swears not only loyalty to my crown, but to the freedom I have in choosing who I'm going to marry! Got it?

SIMON   If that is your priority, Majesty.

    SIMON *goes.* MARY *turns to* SUSAN.

MARY   You didn't say if Bess was in on this.

SUSAN   We thought the rebellion was enough bad news to get you out of bed.

MARY   Shit.

BASSETT   That's the rebels' goal.

MARY   What is.

BASSETT   To take the city and put Bess on the throne.

SUSAN   / You have to deal with her.

BASSETT   You have to deal with her.

MARY   Okay, okay.

    A moment.

Okay. Let's bring her in.

* * *

At table. MARY *writes while in private* BESS *reads* MARY's *letter.*

MARY Right dear and entirely beloved sister,
We greet you well. And whereas certain evil-disposed persons do induce an unnatural rebellion against the tranquility of our realm: We,

BOTH tendering the safety of your person,

BESS which might chance to be in some peril if any sudden danger should arise where you are, or about Donnington Castle, whither, as we understand, you are minded shortly to remove, we think it expedient you should make your repair hither to us. Which we pray you . . .

BOTH *Fail. Not. To do.*

MARY Assuring you, that you may most *safely* remain here, and be most heartily welcome to us. And of your mind herein, we pray you to return answer post-haste.

 A moment.

Your loving sister, Mary the queen.

 MARY *looks up from the letter.* BESS *looks up from the letter.*

BESS Fiddlesticks.

* * *

> *At table.* MARY *stands in uniform at the head of the situation room.* SUSAN *is with* MARY *as she reviews files of "intelligence." The air in the room is taut and not without fear.*

SUSAN Look, you had every reason to trust in the loyalty of Thomas Wyatt—

MARY *(adamant)* I shouldn't trust anyone.

SUSAN Me, pumpkin. Trust me.

MARY *(blasting her)* You're not on the front line in Kent with a musket!
Bess is right.

SUSAN Not very often.

MARY I'm just not good at this.

SUSAN You couldn't know the London guard would mutiny to Wyatt's cause.

> BASSETT *enters on the run with new intelligence reports.* MARY *reads these as* BASSETT *and* SUSAN *continue their disagreement.*

BASSETT The rebels have crossed at Richmond.

SUSAN Now just hold your horses, Miss Bassett. You are not gonna come storming in here and put my queen in another impossible situation.

BASSETT It's a situation. Whether it's impossible we'll soon / see.

SUSAN No. No. No, we will not.

MARY Susan—

SUSAN	*(to MARY)* Now, you just listen to me, young lady: you did not become the first queen of England just so they could run you off a cliff.
BASSETT	We can beat them.
SUSAN	Sure. You say that. You have no loyalty.
BASSETT	No loyal/ty—?!
SUSAN	Doesn't matter who wears the crown, as long as you have your hand in.

> *SUSAN shakes her head and moves away. BASSETT redirects her steam, engages MARY in the report.*

BASSETT	We managed to turn them back from London Bridge yesterday. Now they're mobilizing in Richmond *(on the map)* and splitting their ranks to march north and south around the park.
SUSAN	They'll be right outside the window!
MARY	We'll duck. *(back to BASSETT)* Do we have enough guns to defend the city gates?
BASSETT	Yeah, but we'll need cannons at the bridges.
MARY	How many troops do they have?
BASSETT	Over four thousand. Plus the turncoat London guards.
MARY	Dammit.
BASSETT	You underestimated the political sympathies of the urban soldiers, that's all.
MARY	Yeah! How do I get out of it?
BASSETT	It's too late now to get your rural base activated. The only hope we have is mobilizing the city's liberals.
SUSAN	Time to retreat.

BASSETT	/ No!
MARY	No! I'm not going to retreat! I'm going to make a speech at the Guildhall and win them over.

SIMON enters, clipboard in hand. There is a taut energy between SIMON and SUSAN.

	(to SIMON) Has the Council sent a team of negotiators to Wyatt?
SIMON	Not the wisest policy, / Your—
MARY	*My* policy, Simon! Do it! Tell the traitors that if they lay down their weapons they will be pardoned.

SIMON is not in the mood.

SIMON	If you had handled Jane and Elizabeth the day you took the throne, you would have completely averted this threat!
MARY	Stop telling me how I've screwed up and help me!
SIMON	Declare war.
MARY	On my own people? Don't be stupid.
SIMON	*(aside)* Bienheureuse / Marie. *[Blessed Mary.]*
MARY	You're a diplomat, Simon. You should know better.

SIMON swallows his frustration. BASSETT takes MARY's side.

BASSETT	*(to SIMON)* Send the negotiator. If Wyatt can turn our people, we can turn his.
MARY	Thank you. *(adamantly, to SIMON)* Offer them forgiveness. It'll at least make them think twice.

SIMON places a letter in front of MARY.

SIMON	Elizabeth has sent her reply.
MARY	She's left Hatfield?

MARY opens the letter.

SUSAN   Oughta be here soon, then.

MARY   Ah.

      MARY tosses the letter, as if it's burning her fingers, onto the table.

      Hah. Not coming.

BASSETT   What?

SUSAN   That little bitch.

      SUSAN takes the letter and reads it. MARY is rattled.

MARY   I told her to come.

BASSETT   She should come.

SUSAN   Unable to move, she says.

SIMON   *(with a barely perceptible raise of the eyebrow)* A female complaint?

SUSAN   *(to SIMON)* Now, you just—

BASSETT   "The best possible excuse not to do what you're told."

MARY   *(agreeing with SUSAN)* That little bitch.

SUSAN   *(to MARY)* Retreat. We can get you to Windsor, and if not there, the Tower.

MARY   This is my job!

BASSETT   If their queen has fled, what will the Londoners be fighting for?

SUSAN   A queen who's still alive!

MARY   *(still on BESS)* Sick, my ass. What's her part in all of this?

SIMON   Elizabeth is leading a conspiracy to take your crown!

SUSAN   A pretty good reason to stay away.

BASSETT	A very good reason to head to Donnington Castle: far better to oversee a coup from a fortress than a manor house.
SIMON	Chit-chat, chit-chat! There are rebels on the way!
MARY	All right already, Simon! *(giving orders)* Guns and cannons in defensive positions. Negotiators to the front. I'll head to the Guildhall to rally some support.

MARY signs the orders on SIMON's clipboard and hands them back. SIMON, SUSAN, and BASSETT go.

* * *

In public. MARY rouses support at the Guildhall.

MARY	*(with anxious determination)* At my coronation when I was wedded to the realm *(holds up her finger with the state ring)* you promised your allegiance and obedience to me. And this I say to you in the word of a prince: I cannot tell how naturally the mother loves the child, for I was never the mother of any, but certainly, if a prince and governor may as naturally and earnestly love her subjects as the mother doth the child, then assure yourselves that I do as earnestly and as tenderly love and favour you. And I cannot but think that you as heartily and faithfully love me: and so I doubt not, but we shall give these rebels a short and speedy overthrow.

As concerns the Spanish marriage: I assure you, I am not so willful, neither so affectionate, that either for mine own pleasure I would choose where I lust, or even that I would needs *have* a marriage. I have hitherto lived a virgin, and doubt not, that with God's grace, I would be happy to live still.

But, if it please God that I might leave some fruits of my body behind me as an *heir* to my estate, I trust you would not only rejoice thereat, but also I know it would be to your great comfort as a people. Thus in the word of a queen I promise you: if I did think or know that this marriage were to hurt any of you, my commons, or that it shall not be for the high benefit and commodity of all the whole realm, then I will abstain from marriage while I live.

My father, King Henry, possessed the same regal state which now rightly is descended unto me: and to him always you showed yourselves most faithful and loving subjects, and therefore I doubt not but you will show yourselves likewise unto me. Now then, pluck up your hearts and stand fast against Wyatt and these rebels, both my enemies and yours, and fear them not: for I assure you, I fear them nothing at all, and I will stand with you for your defence!

* * *

At table. MARY *is back in the situation room.* SIMON, SUSAN, *and* BASSETT *enter.*

BASSETT Wyatt's been taken at Ludgate!

MARY He's— / What?

BASSETT His followers were stopped at Charing Cross by thousands of people rallying in the square.
The rebellion is down. The conspirators arrested and heading to the Tower.

MARY I don't know how we— Civilian casualties?

BASSETT None.

MARY can't quite take it in. She sits.

MARY   Huh. We did it.

SIMON   Your Majesty has prevailed.

SUSAN   Well, we can thank the good Lord for that.

MARY   We did it.

> *MARY sits and slumps back in the chair for a moment. But SIMON is not ready to rest.*

SIMON   It is now imperative that you undertake sentencing for the perpetrators and contend with those rebels still at large.

MARY   *(resentful)* Can't you pat me on the back for just a second?

> *SUSAN makes a move to comfort MARY.*

SUSAN   I will—

> *SIMON stops her.*

SIMON   *(adamant)* Wyatt and his rebels are merely the ones who showed their hand.

MARY   *(raising her head)* All the guilty parties will get what's coming to them.

SIMON   Then arrest Elizabeth.

MARY   You're raining on my / parade!

SIMON   Elizabeth has staged an attempted coup!

MARY   Fine. If Bess won't come to me of her own accord, send a delegation to accompany her on the journey.
          (to SIMON) Okay?

> *BASSETT takes note.*

SIMON   To the Tower. On charges of treason.

MARY   Oh, for the love of Andy, everybody thinks it's so fucking straightforward.
          (a little temper) Didn't I just say?! Bring her in!

MARY signs the orders on BASSETT's clipboard. SIMON squares for a heated debate.

SIMON My concern—and the concern of much of the Council and the Commons—is that you have been given this authority by the people but you won't use it.

MARY Justice involves *clemency*.

SIMON In balance with *retribution*. But perhaps retribution does not sit so easily in a woman's province?

MARY Whoa, Nellie Dean. I hope it doesn't sit easily in anyone's *province*. My father was King and so am I.

MARY grabs the clipboard from BASSETT and writes down her own orders.

"Gallows . . . at all the gates . . . *and* in all the squares of the city . . . Hang the turncoat London guards . . . in the doorways of their houses."

MARY hands the order to SIMON.

Is that butch enough for you?

SIMON *(not satisfied)* And what of your sister?

INHERITANCE

In between. CATALINA and MARY, who is pacing like a caged animal.

CATALINA Do it! Do it, for the love of God! Get the kitten out of the way and deal with the wolf!

MARY Oh, crap—now just hang on a minute there, Mother: you are not in my shoes!! You can talk a blue streak about what you would do if you held the magic wand, but I actually have it in my hand! It's a scary little weapon!

CATALINA You know what has to be done.

MARY Shut up! I *do* know what has to be done!

CATALINA Then—?

MARY Oh, Jesus, I can't breathe.

CATALINA Sit.

MARY I can't breathe.

CATALINA Put your head between your knees.

MARY That hurts my stomach. Don't . . . touch me.

CATALINA I'm trying to / help you.

MARY Just . . . I can't breathe!!

CATALINA I / don't— [know how to help you].

MARY I'm lying down.

CATALINA On the floor?

MARY On the table. I'm lying on the table.

CATALINA Are you breathing now?

MARY *(barely)* This much.
Don't look at me.

CATALINA I'm not.

MARY You are. I can feel you.

In her mind MARY *turns* CATALINA *away.*

That's better.

MARY *stares at the ceiling. Winces.*

I have to kill my cousin.

CATALINA Do I respond?

MARY   No. You just— No.
I know that I have to kill my cousin.
I don't want to kill my cousin.
She's nice.
She's, well, she's like me. Not that I'm nice, but that—I can
see the similarities. And someone who has been through
what I have been through deserves a second chance. A third
chance. As many chances as it takes.
But because I hold the wand, that's not a good enough
reason to give her that chance. Because *she* is in prison and
I hold the wand, and if I let her out of prison she can take
the wand, or at least people think she can take the wand . . .
and the fact that I understand her, have compassion for—*get*
her, isn't enough of a reason.
Not when I hold the wand.
And putting it off just makes the wand heavier. And then I
know I have to use the stupid wand, and I wish I had used
it earlier and gotten it over with because now the weight is
too heavy and I can't breathe from holding it up.

A moment.

I'm glad I've . . . What's the word? Lay? Lain? Laid?
Whatever. I like the table. I'd like to just stay here on the
table.

A moment.

CATALINA   Can I speak now?

MARY   But I'll stop you if you say shit that I don't want to hear.
Clear?

CATALINA   Clear.

MARY   What. Then.

CATALINA   Elizabeth.

MARY   Yup.

CALINA Why are you—?

MARY Stop. [I know what you want to know.]
(slowly) Am I keeping Jane alive . . . because if I have to kill
Jane . . . then I sure as hell have to kill Bess.

CATALINA Are you?

MARY Of course I am! I've lived with that little weirdo her whole
life. If I release the hounds on Jane—who is totally naive,
may I add, a *disciple*, who is *seriously* innocent—how the
hell can I justify keeping my hands off the evil genius?

CATALINA You can't.

MARY Right. And then . . . ? Who's next. Father was killing at
random by the end. Without conscience.

CATALINA You will never do that. You will only kill with knowledge
and with purpose.

MARY He's remembered as a goddamn hero; you think I will be?
And what if something goes wrong? Another
Margaret Pole—
Oh, shit! You don't know! You were already dead!

CATALINA What happened to Margaret Pole?

MARY Eleven blows from the executioner.

CATALINA Madre de / Dios. *[Mother of God.]*

> *MARY rises on her elbows to look directly at CATALINA.*

MARY Gory. Hacked my nanny's head to bits. Right down to her
sternum. She was still screaming ten minutes in.

> *MARY goes back to lying on the table and looking up.*

Jeepers. What if that happens to Jane?
Or to . . .

CATALINA You cannot be held responsible for the skill of the
executioner.

MARY   No. My culpability is over once the *paper* is signed. Henry was like, rack 'em up: eighteen people for opposing him politically, ten for sleeping around on him, three of his closest religious advisors, one for loving his wife and daughter, one for homosexuality, one for feminism. And . . . poor Surrey.

CATALINA   Why Surrey?

MARY   Didn't like his outfit. *(off with his head)* Whmpff.

> *MARY suddenly buckles with a sharp pain in her guts.*

Go ahead! Eat me alive!! I'm still going to do it!

CATALINA   You are Henry's heir.

MARY   I am Henry's heir. *I* am Henry's heir!

CATALINA   Mi ratóncita.

> *MARY bites down the pain and leaps off the table.*

MARY   Ready the block.

CHAPTER 13

> *In private. JANE stands in her shift in a prison cell. On the table are two black dresses, Katherine Parr's prayer book, and three letters. MARY is with her, agitated. They are considering the dresses.*

JANE   Which one do you think?

MARY   They're both black.

JANE   They're the best I have. I want you to have something from me.

MARY   Okay. I . . . like the one with the jet buttons.

JANE I wore that one to my trial.

MARY The other one then.

JANE No. You're right. The one with the buttons.

>*JANE smiles at MARY.*

We have similar taste.

>*MARY sets her jaw. Then releases it. JANE looks out the window at the scaffold.*

I'm allowed witnesses.

MARY Of course.

JANE Mrs. Ellen, then: my nurse. And Mrs. Tylney, who stayed with me in the Tower.

MARY You bet.

>*JANE takes Katherine Parr's prayer book and ties it around her waist. Her hands are noticeably shaking.*

JANE To dispose of my body . . . they'll need . . . permission.

MARY They'll have it.

JANE Mrs. Tylney says the guards desecrate the bodies of traitors.

>*JANE looks at the scaffold again.*

I've never been naked with a man. I don't want anyone to touch my body but my friends.

MARY It'll all be decent. Promise.

JANE Is that why you come? To reassure me?

>*A silence. MARY turns to leave.*

Is it *you* that takes the greetings to my family?

MARY I can.

>*JANE hands MARY the letters.*

JANE	Here then. For my sisters. For my father.

MARY shuffles the letters.

MARY	And your mother?

JANE says nothing. A silence. MARY turns again.

JANE	Why do you come to see me, Mary?

MARY stops.

(finding her courage) You changed the rules. Mid-game. You gave me false hope.

MARY turns back.

MARY	*(frustrated)* Convert, okay? Just do it! Dudley converted at the end.
JANE	*(losing all her composure) Dudley*?! He converted because he thought it might bring him a pardon.
MARY	If he could try it, can't / you?
JANE	That horrible man made nothing but misery for me! And I'll tell you what: some people think that the piper can change his tune, but I am not one of those people.
MARY	Don't you want to / live!
JANE	*(anger rising)* How could a man that led a life that odious possibly hope for pardon?
MARY	We all deserve mercy.
JANE	Not him! He was a thief and a bully and a *JUDAS*. Convert? Would I give up my faith in order to live another day? Would you?
MARY	No.
JANE	God forbid I should convert. How can any intelligent person believe that bread is actually the body of Christ our Lord, when it was made in the kitchen by the baker.

My soul is not so fickle.

I took responsibility, but I'm not guilty. I'm no Dudley. I'm *sixteen*; I have my whole pure and good life before me! But do you see me begging you for mercy? Do you? *Do* you?

MARY   / No.

JANE   No!

Dudley was a hypocrite. He was willing to betray his saviour for a pardon.

MARY   Life is sweet.

JANE   A sweet life cannot buy salvation. Today, I go to paradise. If I deny my faith, my God won't recognize me. I broke a temporal law, I will not break a divine one.

MARY   No. You'll leave that to me.

JANE   Take comfort, Mary. I go to love. *(loosely quoting scripture)* In my heart, I have faith: faith that can move mountains, but until I know love, I know nothing. I can willingly deliver my body to the fire, but—

MARY   Wait.

Say that again?

JANE   I can willingly deliver my body to the fire—

MARY   To the *fire*? *(considering this)* I'd forgotten that part . . .

JANE   —but without love, I am nothing.

MARY   "I am nothing . . . "

JANE   The grace of God is there for you, too, Mary.

MARY   Ha. You're a brave girl.

JANE   You give me courage.

MARY   I'll suffer for this.

JANE   I wouldn't want to be in your shoes.

MARY   You go to your God.

JANE   I'm so grateful you say that.
        You've always been so kind to me.

BLOCKHEAD

*In between. MARY sits in stillness. Another location in pri-
vate: an executioner's block. JANE enters in her shift. She
has a white handkerchief in one hand and Katherine Parr's
prayer book tied around her waist. Both MARY and JANE
kneel. MARY echoes JANE's prayer in Latin.*

JANE   Have mercy upon me, O God: according unto the multi-
        tude of thy tender mercies: / wash me, and I shall be whiter
        than snow.
        Create in me a clean heart, O God; then will I teach trans-
        gressors thy ways, and sinners shall be converted unto thee.

MARY   Miserere mei Deus secundum magnam misericordiam tuam
        et secundum multitudinem miserationum.
        Cor mundum crea in me Deus; docebo iniquos vias tuas et
        impii ad te convertentur.

        *Both MARY and JANE stand. A HOODED FIGURE enters to
        the block. Stands beside JANE. JANE begins to untie her shift.
        Her hands fumble. The figure steps in to help.*

        Let her alone.

        JANE bares her shoulders and her neck.

HOODED
FIGURE Do you forgive me, Madam?

MARY   She forgives you. Do it quickly.

        JANE falters in fear. She holds out the handkerchief.

JANE	Will you take it off before I lay me down?
HOODED FIGURE	No, Madam.

JANE ties the handkerchief around her eyes. She can't find her way to the block.

JANE	Where is it? Where is it? *(panicking)* What shall I do?
MARY	Help her! For God's sake.

The HOODED FIGURE steps forward. She guides JANE to the block. JANE kneels and places her head onto the block.

JANE	Lord, into thy hands I commend my spirit.

JANE thrusts her arms out to her sides. We hear the axe fall. The HOODED FIGURE reveals herself.

CATALINA	So perish all the queen's enemies.

THE TIDE TURNS

In private. SUSAN is dressing MARY in JANE's black dress.

In public. In another location, BASSETT leads BESS down a narrow walkway toward the Tower. BESS's hands are bound.

BESS	She wouldn't. She promised. Mary would never just chuck me in the Tower without hearing my side of the story.
BASSETT	The queen refuses to see you.
BESS	I'm not a criminal. I'm a patriot.
BASSETT	Patriot? Is that how you're promoting yourself?
BESS	You want me to swear? I'll swear.

BESS holds up the crucifix from around her neck.

See this. I swear on this . . . that I never said or agreed to anything that might put Mary or our country in any danger.

BASSETT   What good is the oath of a person who believes nothing?

BESS   *(raging at the subordinate)* Tell her! Tell her I want to talk to *her*, not you. Tell her I have to see her before I go to the Tower.
(equivocating) If it's possible, I mean.
I have to see Mary before any of this gets out. Before you persuade people to think I'm guilty, before you even know what I've done. Where's your proof?

BASSETT   We know one of Wyatt's cohorts advised you to move your household to the higher security of Donnington Castle.

BESS   Never heard of it.

BASSETT   Let me stimulate your memory: it's a secure rallying location for your French allies and your pals in the southwest, who would be only too happy to support the incursion you had initiated.

> BESS *feels the onslaught of evidence coming and calls for the judge and jury.*

BESS   *(up to* MARY*)* Mary! Mary, listen to me! I know you're up there. I'm sorry to be throwing my weight around. I wouldn't be doing this if I had anything to hide, and you've always been so good to me, and isn't there a chance that I'm innocent? All I want is for you to allow me that chance.

> *She glances at* BASSETT.

You have to hear it from me. You have to believe *me*.

BASSETT   There's no one there.

BESS   These *people* are going to try to turn one sister against the other. They don't understand our bond.

> BESS *kneels.*

Can you see me? I'm kneeling now. I'm bowing to you. Please? Let me in. Everyone thinks you hate me, but you don't hate me. I know that. I wouldn't even ask if I had one doubt that I can clear my name.

BASSETT   We have evidence of your participation in the conspiracy from Wyatt himself.

BESS   *(to MARY)* Okay, Wyatt? Maybe he did . . . write me a note, but seriously, I never got it.

BASSETT   The French envoy was caught carrying a letter of yours to the king of France.

BESS   *(to MARY)* Okay, the . . . the letter that was found with the courier, I don't even understand how it came into existence. I mean, I never sent the French king anything, of any kind, and if that's not the truth, I'll die for it. Swear.

It starts to rain. Fed up, BASSETT exits.

C'mon, Mary. Please let me talk to you.

There is nothing but silence and stillness.

Donnington Castle? Is that the name? It, it, it could be that I've seen it on a . . . list of my properties.

More silence.

Don't put me in the Tower. My mother was there before she died. I can't go in that tower as a prisoner. Don't make me.

BESS sinks to the ground. SIMON enters.

SIMON   You should come in. No point sitting out in the rain.

BESS   Better sitting here than in a worse place.

SIMON helps BESS up, takes her by the elbow, and leads her off.

MOMENTARILY OUT OF ACTION

> *At bed. MARY stands apart. She is wearing JANE's dress.*
>
> *SUSAN sits at a distance.*
>
> *BASSETT enters. She carries a small jewellery box in her hand, which we barely see. BASSETT looks at MARY, expecting no response. She goes to SUSAN.*

SUSAN   Is he coming?

BASSETT   His father's about to abdicate. Philip will have an entire empire to oversee.

SUSAN   Is he coming?

BASSETT   He's got more important things on his mind.
He wants her to know he likes the gifts she sent, especially the jewelled poniard.

SUSAN   Nothing wins a man's heart like a jewelled poniard, I always say.

BASSETT   He's not coming.

SUSAN   No.

> *A moment.*

BASSETT   There's a gift from him.

SUSAN   One?

BASSETT   Here.

> *BASSETT reveals the little box.*

MARY   *(distant)* What is it?

BASSETT   *(surprised at MARY's response)* Oh.
Why don't you open it?

SUSAN   *(trying to provide levity)* What do you think, a necktie? Pair of socks?

MARY   *(without moving)* You open it.

> *BASSETT opens the box and both she and SUSAN look inside.*

BASSETT   It's. Small.

SUSAN   It is. Small.

BASSETT   Delicate.

SUSAN   Yes.

BASSETT   Pretty.

SUSAN   Absolutely.

BASSETT   Put it on.

> *MARY doesn't move. BASSETT takes out a very pretty, delicate bracelet set with small diamonds. SUSAN goes to MARY and puts the bracelet on MARY's wrist.*

SUSAN   Delicate.

BASSETT   Pretty.

SUSAN   Small.

> *A moment. MARY holds out her wrist, looking at the bracelet.*

MARY   I killed my cousin for this.

> *A moment. SIMON enters.*

BASSETT   Not now, Simon.

SIMON   *(bowing)* Prince Philip sends greetings to his loving aunt.

SUSAN   He's gonna have to stop calling her that pretty soon.

SIMON   The prince also asks me to convey a directive—a . . . request . . .

MARY   What . . . request?

SIMON	He asks that Elizabeth be released from the Tower.
SUSAN	For Pete's sake: you're the one who put her in there! You've been harping for months about it, and now—?
SIMON	As the prince's arrival on English soil approaches, there are more pressing security concerns that must be taken into consideration.
SUSAN	What about *Mary's* security concerns. I suppose they're none of Phil's business?
SIMON	Prince Philip feels that if anything . . . untoward . . . should happen to Elizabeth while she's incarcerated, the English people would immediately blame the Spanish influence over the queen, and thereby weaken his authority.
SUSAN	She's been doing this for him!
SIMON	He won't set foot in England until such possibilities have been eliminated.
MARY	Go on.
SIMON	Certainly, Your Majesty: the prince has suggested a marriage contract for your sister. He believes it would be advantageous to all concerned if Elizabeth was to marry. And in preparation for this proposal, you should set her free.
MARY	Release her then.
BASSETT	What?! No— You can't just marry her off. What happened to no woman being a commodity?
MARY	Speak with the Tower warden.
SIMON	The prince will be pleased with your concession.
	SIMON goes.
BASSETT	What is going on with you? You can't just do what he says!
MARY	*(coldly and clearly to BASSETT)* Let. Bess. Out.

BASSETT   *(cowed)* I'll speak with the Tower warden.

> *BASSETT goes. MARY looks at her bracelet.*

MARY   If I'd chosen an Englishman, there never would have been a rebellion; Jane could have lived.

SUSAN   Maybe.

> *A moment.*

MARY   Susan?

SUSAN   Yes, Mouse.

MARY   What if I'm too old?

SUSAN   Men like older women.

MARY   Men like older women because they have experience. They like younger women 'cause they have none.
I'm neither of the women men like.
Bess is all the women men like: she wreaks of fecundity.

SUSAN   Bully for her.

MARY   She'll make a great wife. A great mother.

SUSAN   Then get her married. Out of your hair. Far enough away that she can't suddenly walk off with your husband.

MARY   Philip'll like her. And she'll see the value in him.

> *A moment.*

I know you know.

SUSAN   What?

MARY   What Phil says about me.

SUSAN   It doesn't bear repeating.

MARY   That it would take God himself to drink this cup.

CAUGHT IN THE DEVIL'S BARGAIN

> *In private.* MARY *and* BESS *are in a holding room. They are at each other.*

BESS You think I would treat you like this?

MARY Go on then! Tell me what you were gonna do to me if your rebellion had succeeded. Exile? Execution? / Worse?

BESS *Two months* I was in that / damp—

MARY Chicken.

BESS —horrible tower. And where are you sending me now?

MARY Woodstock.

BESS To kill me. In secret.

MARY Oh, for pity's sake.

BESS I did nothing wrong.

MARY Don't start.

BESS It's true.

MARY I know you! Don't forget that! And even though no hare-brained scheme is beyond you, I said, "Nope, I need *proof* to raise a hand against my *sister*." And wouldn't you know it . . . there is none.

BESS I told you—

MARY Don't interrupt me!

BESS Sorry.

MARY Wyatt cleared you. Aren't you lucky. Just before his head came off. He said you and Courtenay were just pictures on the poster; that neither of you played a part in the actual plot.

BESS   You believe him?

MARY   There's no reliable evidence to the contrary.
          So you're out.

BESS   But I'm not free.

MARY   Because there are already pamphlets circulating—with your
          name on them!—calling for the next uprising!
          House arrest at Woodstock is a transitional measure.

BESS   Another prison.

MARY   A comfortable isolation.

BESS   Payback.

MARY   It's not.

BESS   Because my mother did it to your mother.

MARY   It's not vengeance.

BESS   Looks like it. Smells like it. Tastes like it.

MARY   I did it for Philip.

BESS   You. What?

MARY   Otherwise he wouldn't come.

BESS   Oh! So he's the boss already!

MARY   Hey! I need him in the vicinity, don't I? if I'm going to get
          pregnant?

BESS   You don't need to. I'm your heir.

MARY   Over my dead body.

BESS   You mean I'm in prison until you have a kid?!

MARY   *Out* of prison. That's the point.

          MARY tentatively plays her card.

          Or . . . there is an option.

BESS   What.

MARY   Maybe. I. Have a marriage proposal for you.

BESS   You— No way.

MARY   The Duke of / Savoy—

BESS   No. Wayyyy. I thought, I *thought* . . . when you were *Queen*,
you weren't going to bargain away any more cherry.

MARY   / Hey.

BESS   I *thought* with a woman at the helm . . .
Hah! Women beware women.

MARY   Marry the damned Duke of Savoy! It's an advantageous
match.

BESS   For your political purposes.

MARY   One that Henry would approve of; one that'll keep you safe
and healthy so you can have children who will contribute
to the economic and political stability / of the—

BESS   Border security! SMACK!
It comes to this.
I'm not going to marry the Duke of Savoy!

MARY   Just do it, will ya?

BESS   So you feel better about killing Jane Grey?

MARY   Shut up.

BESS   You've just put down a rebellion on the grounds that every
woman should have the right to choose her own husband,
and now you're going to crawl right back up the ass of the
patriarchy and force me into bed with Europe?
Mary. Come on. It's laughable.

MARY   Yup. Laugh at me. Fuck. I don't know. I can't do this job.
You have to be a complete asshole to do this job.

BESS	I won't agree to your arranged marriage. So . . . I guess I'm going to my comfortable prison at Woodstock.
MARY	You'll be safe there.
BESS	For how long?
MARY	Until I'm pregnant and the nation has that kind of stability.
BESS	Isn't that exactly what you told Jane?
MARY	Don't. Don't! The sooner you admit what we both know: that you want my job and you'll do anything in your power to get it, including putting your face forward as a poster child for the goddamned rebels!!—when you *admit* that you want me gone, that you want my *faith* gone, then—THEN I'll set you free. Deal?
BESS	Do me a favour?
MARY	What.
BESS	Kill me with a sword, not an axe. I want to die like my mother died. Confessing *nothing*.

WHAT'S AT STAKE

In between. MARY *and* CATALINA. MARY *clutches at her belly in pain.*

MARY	Damn it. Damn it!
CATALINA	Kill her.
MARY	My guts are falling out here, okay? What the hell is wrong with / me?
CATALINA	All the women who have come before you—why did they trample the path if you are unwilling to take / it?
MARY	Unwilling?!

CATALINA   If you kill her the country will join behind you and your legal status as monarch.

MARY   *You* may think that. I—don't know what to think. And if I can't figure out how to operate in the current political climate, I'm sure as hell not going to listen to a woman who died of melodrama twenty years ago!

CATALINA   Don't you speak to me like / that—

MARY   You're so certain you know what's right. Well, I'm not your daughter then, because I . . . I . . . have nothing but *un*certainty.

CATALINA   Find your conviction.

MARY   I did! I killed my cousin!

CATALINA   Kill Elizabeth.

MARY   No!

CATALINA   Take my conviction.

MARY   NO! I like my *scruples*, thank you very much, and I'm stickin' by 'em.

CATALINA   If you kill Elizabeth, you will be remembered forever as the one who healed the rift, who repaired the schism.

MARY   If she dies—if I have her killed—if I *kill* her—I won't last five minutes on the throne, lawful Queen or not:
I kill my sister, I kill myself.
I. Have. No. Heir.

CATALINA   We must not think about that.

MARY   *(pushing CATALINA)* You better think about that.

> ANNE *steps forward from the shadows.*

Great. / You want a piece of me, too.

CATALINA   *(under her breath)* Sancta Maria, Mater Dei. *[Holy Mary, mother of God.]*

ANNE   Are you ready to give up?

MARY   Piss off.

ANNE   Elizabeth is your heir.

MARY   Not if I have a kid.

CATALINA   *(to ANNE)* You do not know what the future will bring.

ANNE   *(to MARY)* What are the odds?
(to CATALINA) How blessed was the fruit of *your* womb? How many times did you cry out?
To what end?

MARY   Me. I am the end.

ANNE   *(to MARY)* You *are* the end. Feel your belly.

> ANNE *puts* MARY's *hand to her belly.* MARY *buckles in pain.*

CATALINA   *(starting toward MARY)* Do not lay your hand upon my child!

MARY   *(stopping her)* Mamá: listen to her.

ANNE   Do you feel that?

MARY   *(to ANNE)* Since I was twelve.

CATALINA   *(starting toward MARY again)* You did not inherit my inadequate womb!

MARY   I said stop! She's here for a reason.

ANNE   Is it hard to the touch?
Is there blood, blood, and more blood?

CATALINA   Bruja! *[Witch!]*

ANNE   *(to CATALINA)* No, honey, I'm just an ordinary woman who got caught.
(matter of fact, to MARY) Are you your mother's daughter?

MARY hesitates.

You know the answer. You've known for years. No heir to the throne could ever survive in such a hostile environment.

MARY No.

MARY turns to CATALINA.

I am my mother's daughter.

CATALINA You are not!

ANNE *(as she goes)* Elizabeth is your heir.

CATALINA This is not your destiny!

MARY Anne's right.

CATALINA *I* am right!

MARY No. You are not right.
It isn't about destiny; it isn't about blood; it isn't about who comes next. It isn't about you.
You've led me, Mamá, but you had no idea to where.
There's no point in killing my sister. It was never about her.
It's about *my* opportunity. Right now.
It's about Jane Grey, and proving what *I* know is right.

CATALINA retreats into the shadows.

Susan! Bassett! Get in here!
(to CATALINA, who is no longer there) Mamá: I survived. Of all your children, I survived.

SUSAN enters.

SUSAN Mouse?

MARY *(calling)* Simon!

BASSETT enters from another location.

BASSETT Can you take notes?
I'll get a pen.

MARY	Do you remember Henry's Act of the Six Articles?
BASSETT	Not easy to forget.
MARY	Can you bring a copy, please.

BASSETT withdraws.

SUSAN	You need help?
MARY	Susan . . . *(decisively)* I'm not gonna give up. I haven't come this far to give up.
SUSAN	I'm right there with you, my girlie-girl.

BASSETT re-enters.

BASSETT	The Act of the Six Articles, as requested.
MARY	Thank you.
BASSETT	Notebook. Pen. Ready.

SIMON enters from another location with his handy clipboard.

SIMON	*(bowing)* Your Majesty.
MARY	Come in, Simon. Sit down.

SUSAN hesitates.

All of you.

BASSETT, SUSAN, and SIMON take their seats at the conference table. MARY is at the head, working it out.

I've been waiting for all this to make sense—you've been very patient. I've been protecting my heart; you've watched me do it.
The heart is weak. The heart doesn't go to battle. The heart can't be King.

(facts) There have been women before me, and there will be women after me; women who don't shrink from the sight of blood; women who argue; women who kill. Women who cling to what they believe, right or wrong. For years, if that's what it takes. Till death, if that's what it takes. My mother did that. I am my mother's daughter.

A moment.

Right. Let's talk policy.

BASSETT   Yes, yes, yes, I love this part.

MARY   I was too lenient in my first parliament.

SUSAN   Don't be hard on yourself.

BASSETT   The moderate stance just didn't pay off.

MARY   My good intentions weren't strong enough to deter Wyatt.

SIMON   A lesson learned: ambiguity leads to chaos.

MARY   No more ambiguity.
(to SIMON) Eddie's Protestant policy is still on the books, right?

SIMON   It is.

MARY   Abolish it; I want to repeal all of Eddie's religious legislation and reinstate Henry's response to the changes coming from Europe.

SIMON   Easily done, Your Majesty.

MARY   We're going back to Henry's church, before the chaos.

SUSAN   Before the Lutherans.

BASSETT   *(looking in the table of contents)* Just a sec. Just a sec. It's here somewhere. Yes: *(showing them)* here's the bill: "An Act Abolishing Diversity in Opinions."

MARY   That actually sounds very useful. Very simple: one faith, one doctrine. Let's revisit that.

SIMON   Is it your wish to restore the power of the papacy, Your Majesty?

MARY   I think we should start the conversation with Rome.

SUSAN   Good.

BASSETT   Very good.

MARY   *(to BASSETT)* And there were heresy laws, too, weren't there? Part of that same legislative bill?

BASSETT   Yes . . .

MARY   They'll act as a deterrent for the predictable opposition.

BASSETT   Here: *(reading)* " . . . and that every such offender shall therefore have and suffer judgment, execution, pain, and pains of death by way of burning, without any abjuration, clergy, or sanctuary to be therefore permitted, had, allowed, admitted, or suffered."

SUSAN   That oughta do it.

SIMON   A very effective means of demonstrating religious authority and political impunity.

MARY   I will show as much authority and impunity as any good king does.
How many deaths will that take?

BASSETT   A half-dozen or so and you're rid of the worst culprits.

MARY   Power and tyranny over right and justice, yes, Simon?

SIMON   That is the best course in leadership, Your Majesty.
And I agree with Bassett—

BASSETT   You're slipping, Simon.

SIMON —regarding the numbers: a few prominent leaders first, and after that a few subordinates. Enough to destabilize their followers and bring their loyalty back to us. You. The personal security of all your subjects lies with you.

SUSAN You want to live in this country, you follow the rules of this country. That's how it should be.

MARY The victims of Henry's divorce may believe something completely different from what you and I believe, but they have a choice, and in that choice, we're the same: some will accept death willingly for the life of their soul.
Jane did. I would, too. I would stand in the flames myself if the shoe was on the other foot.

BASSETT I would stand there with you.

SUSAN We all would.

MARY Jane Grey chose to die. Others will choose to die.

SIMON I'll draft the resolutions for parliament.

SUSAN Courage, Mouse. You're not in this game alone.

MARY Yes, I am. I am the only king at this table. I'm the rightful heir to exactly this. I'm delivering them to the fire. I'm burning the goddamned heretics!

THE DAUGHTER OF TIME

In between. The sun is brightly shining. MARY *walks slowly by. A few moments later* BESS *appears. She looks around. She waits.* MARY *returns, looks around, joins her.*

BESS See the sun shining through the stained glass?

MARY How about that.

BESS   So pretty.

MARY   Uhuh.

    They look up at a large monument in Westminster Abbey.

    Look at you: you got kind of a big tomb there, sister.

BESS   It's not my fault.

MARY   *(incredulous)* You're on top of me!

BESS   I didn't ask for that.

MARY   Seriously. A huge effigy of you in Westminster Abbey, and . . . hmmm . . . *(looking about)* where's the one for Mary?

BESS   It wasn't me; I was dead. It was the Scot—James—he put my coffin on top of yours.

MARY   Obliterated me completely.

BESS   Sorry.

MARY   But not his mother, no! Mary Stuart gets an even bigger tribute right over there, but me? Lost. Buried. Forgotten.

BESS   I gave you a super fancy funeral.

MARY   Small consolation. At least you kept the throne away from the Scottish broad.

BESS   Mary, Mary: so much confusion around the Marys.

MARY   It drives me nuts. *(the monument)* And d'ya think this helps? Nope.

    MARY speaks through a mock megaphone to the crowds.

    The first reigning Queen of England! Get it?! *That* Mary. Not Mary the friggin' Queen of Scots.

BESS   *(through the same megaphone)* BLOODY MARY!

    MARY is stung.

    Sorry.

MARY   Like no one else who ever ran a country was responsible for the death of their enemies.
Or for the death of their own subjects, for that matter.

They look back at the monument.

BESS   I wish there was a surgeon who could open my heart up so that you could see what's really in there; so you could see what I feel, you know, for you.

MARY   You need a surgeon for that?

BESS   All our doctors show us is grief and sickness.

MARY   True.

BESS   Because if you could *see*, then whatever's there *(in my heart)* that's hidden by . . . our . . . you know, being sisters and, well, going through what we had to go through . . . if you could *see*, then that would be *proof.* I could prove that to you. There'd be substance to support it, science. Truth.

A moment.

(slightly too dramatic) And the more the clouds tried to hide the clear light of that truth, the harder that truth would work to push away those clouds.

A moment.

MARY   I don't know how to love.

BESS   I know.

A moment.

MARY   That was a good speech.

BESS   Thanks.

A moment.

MARY   You went a bit too far with the "cloud" stuff.

BESS   Maybe.

MARY   Stick to the science.

BESS   Yeah. Next time I'll leave it at that.

MARY   Smart.

          A moment.

          (without looking at BESS *or offering her hand)* Let's hold hands.

BESS   Really?

          BESS *looks at* MARY. BESS *takes* MARY's *hand. They look at*
          the inscription on the monument.

MARY   How's your Latin?

BESS   Not as good as yours.

MARY   *(reading)* "Regno consortes et urna . . . "

BESS   *(translating)* Partners of reign and grave . . .

MARY   Partners. Could it be more clear?!
          " . . . hic obdormimus Elizabetha et Maria . . . "

BESS   Obdormimus . . . .Here rest. Here *sleep* Elizabeth and
          Mary . . .

MARY   " . . . sorores in spe resurrectionis . . . "

BESS   Sisters in hope . . . of resurrection.

MARY   Too literal. Renewal, maybe. Restoration.

BESS   Oh, I like that: sisters in hope of restoration.

          It's about time.

          The sisters stand without looking at each other.

          Move this way, just a bit. It's warm here.

MARY   Is it ever. Feel the light.

          MARY *and* BESS *remain in the warmth of the sun.* BESS
          fiddles with the crucifix around her neck.

          End of Act Two.

ACKNOWLEDGEMENTS

My thanks to the Stratford Festival, Bob White, Andy McKim, and Alan Dilworth for their support of the dramaturgical and creative development of this work. My thanks to Karon Bales and Charles Beall for their financial support of the premiere productions of *The Last Wife*, *The Virgin Trial*, and *Mother's Daughter*.

The initial stage of this work was created during a residency in the Leighton Artists Studios at the Banff Centre for Arts and Creativity.

My thanks to the actors who worked on this play in development: Sara Farb, Bahia Watson, Irene Poole, Effie Honeywell, Lucy Peacock, Laura Condlin, Sébastien Heins, Shannon Taylor, Shruti Kothari, Carmen Grant, Kim Horsman, Maria Vacratsis, Beryl Bain, Gordon Patrick White, and stage manager Kim Lott.

Kate Hennig is a playwright, actor, teacher, and director. Her play *The Last Wife* premiered at the Stratford Festival in 2015 and has since had more than ten productions across Canada and the United States, and will premiere in Sydney, Australia, in September 2019. *The Virgin Trial* won the 2017 Carol Bolt Award for Best New Play, was shortlisted for the Governor General's Literary Award for Drama, and has had several subsequent regional productions. For the Shaw Festival, Kate has translated and adapted *Cyrano de Bergerac* and Oscar Wilde's stories for children, *Wilde Tales*. Kate is Associate Artistic Director at the Shaw Festival and resides in Stratford, Ontario.